Includes
DVD

VINCENT VERSACE

WELCOME to OZ

A CINEMATIC APPROACH TO

DIGITAL STILL PHOTOGRAPHY WITH PHOTOSHOP

New
Riders

VOICES THAT MATTER

WELCOME TO OZ

A Cinematic Approach to Digital Still Photography with Photoshop

Vincent Versace

New Riders
1249 Eighth Street
Berkeley, CA 94710
510/524-2178
800/283-9444
510/524-2221 (fax)
Find us on the Web at: www.newriders.com

To report errors, please send a note to errata@peachpit.com

New Riders is an imprint of Peachpit, a division of Pearson Education

ISBN 0-7357-1400-2

9 8 7 6 5 4 3 2 1

Printed and bound in the United States of America

To my Father.

Thank you for giving me the childhood you dreamed of.

And

To Tad Z. Danielewski and Sydney Walker.

*Thank you for always being the broom that swept clean and
thank you for teaching me about the gift of giving.*

Acknowledgments

From a grain of sand the pearl comes. —Confucius

One thing I have learned is that writing a book is a collaborative process after which I get all the credit. Which is cool, but...

This book simply would not be this book if it were not for the editorial diligence of Edna A. Elfont, Ph.D. When you read this book and you find that the thoughts are clear, concise, easy to understand, and make sense, that's Edna. If while you are reading this book you find it obtuse and convoluted, and it makes you go "huh?" that's me thinking I know better and not listening to Edna when I should have.

I would not be a photographer if it were not for CJ Elfont, and the technical, photographic accuracy of the book would also not be what it is if it were not for CJ's intervention.

To my brother Lane: I could not have asked for and gotten a better friend than you. To my sister Eve and my mother, I really did win the relative lottery.

I would especially like to thank John Paul Caponigro and Jay Maisel for allowing me to talk them into writing the foreword and afterword of this book, though I suspect they may have done it to shut me up. AND thank you, Peter Bauer, for answering every question I had during the writing process. Peter, you truly have forgotten more than I will ever know about Photoshop. Also great thanks and gratitude go to Sandy Foster, who through no fault of her own became the audience of one. She suffered through every draft of this book. Please know that your insights made for a better book.

Thank you, Challen Cates and Steve Kearin, for all the time you spent sitting in front of my camera waiting for me to get it right. The images of you both make for a much nicer looking book.

To Dave Moser and Scott Kelby, the day you asked me to be a part of the National Association of Photoshop Professionals is the day that led to this book. I never have been more proud to belong to an organization than I am about belonging to NAPP.

To Dan Steinhardt of Epson, thank you for providing me with your unfailing support even when I was a complete pain in the ass. Because of you, a pocket of time was created in which I could create this book.

To Nancy Carr of Kodak, Vincent Park, Anthony Ruotolo of American Photo magazine, Ed Sanchez, Mike Slater of Nik Software, Peter Poremba of Dyna-Lite, Fabia Ochoa of Epson, Tadashi Nakayama, Makoto "Mike" Kimura, Naoki "Santa Claus" Tomino, Richard LoPinto, Mike Rubin, and Mike Corrado of Nikon, Liz Quinlisk of X-Rite, and Richard Rabinowitz: Without all of your faith and support over the years, I would never have had the career that I do.

To Dave Weathers of Technicolor, thank you, thank you, thank you. Where my career is now going is because of you.

Thank you, Robert H. Tourtelot, for never failing to watch out for me.

Thank you, Moose and Sharon Peterson, because of you both, I've been allowed to shoot and see some of the most beautiful places on the earth, which has contributed to chapters in this book.

Thank you, Steve Weiss, for seeing that I really did have a book in me when I really didn't think so.

To Toby, Sally, Adam, and Jamie Rosenblatt: Were it not for you I would have stopped being a photographer.

Thank you to DriveSavers, specifically Jaci Cunningham, Mike Cobb, and Kristina Flanagan, I have no idea how you raised a smoking, 1-terabyte drive from the dead, but if you hadn't in the eleventh hour, this book would never have seen the light of day.

To everyone at Peachpit Press, thank you for your hard work and efforts to make this book happen.

And lastly, to my wife, Sylvia, who has suffered through the writing of this book. You have kept me calm when I was anything but. Lucky for me you have questionable taste in men.

Contents

Foreword

Incoming!

This man is possessed. So is this book. Possessed of a unique perspective. Possessed of an exceptional depth. Possessed of an uncommon passion. Possessed of an unusual compassion for his comrades in creativity.

There are a people out there who want to make the world a better place through photography. This man is one of them. And that's why I'm writing this foreword.

This is a book on photography. Sure it's also a book on Adobe Photoshop, but Vincent is a photographer first, a Photoshop guru second. This brings a specific perspective. It's a perspective that's been lacking in so many books on Photoshop, the de facto digital darkroom. The vast majority of Photoshop books published to date have tried to be everything to everyone; which has generated a pantheon of generic encyclopedias, not unique volumes on craft and vision. This is the latter. Only a handful of publications have a specifically photographic perspective. This is one of the most photographic volumes produced to date.

A religion for some, a lifestyle for many, Vincent considers Photoshop an "imagination enhancer" and a path into new photographic possibilities, but not a substitute for fine photographic craft. He encourages photographers to "act preemptively," to "do it in camera," and to "figure your problems out at the point of capture."

Vincent knows that *why* determines *how*. His philosophy shapes every twist and turn of this book. To fully read a text and grasp all that it has to offer, you need to know the player. Vincent's got specific experience, influences, and passions. And he's willing to disclose it all. He's willing to share everything. Here, you'll find his life story and his ongoing passion

for light. By revealing his thought process he sets you free to choose a different destination, knowledgeably—in part because you've been empowered by the techniques presented in this book.

There are many things you need to know about Vincent Versace.

He's versatile. Vincent Versace suffers from multiple personality disorder. When sitting with Vincent, all manner of heretofore unimaginable combinations reveal themselves; he'll lurch frenetically from the Godfather to Barney in the same breath. (He may be Kaiser Soze.) Then again, he's a trained actor with plenty of experience on the stage, so maybe it's all an act. What a show it is! At first, you might think he's talking with himself. Then you realize he's talking to God. And, he's invited you in to be a part of the conversation. It won't always be lucid but it will be thoroughly engaging. You should have seen the first draft! Whatever this man is on, I want some! Mind you, in small quantities, ingested only at the right times. (Perhaps I should reconsider what I just said. ...)

His presentation is always engaging. Versace wears only Armani. He has one Armani suit for every day of the month. At least his scent is Versace.

He loves life's indulgences. There's Vincent in the morning. Most people who carry a silver spoon consume other substances; Vincent uses his silver spoon for tea. I'm not kidding. Wherever he goes, in addition to a camera, he travels with tea. Stashed in a camera bag you'll find kukicha, spring tea, chrysanthemum oolong, golden dragon oolong, imperial red, bourbon rouge, earl grey with lavender, and his own special blend that includes chocolate. There's Vincent in the evening.

He'll extol the many virtues of single-malt scotch and make nuanced comparisons to Irish whiskey and bourbon, all in the same sitting, practically in the same breath. On any given evening he can always identify what's in my silver flask. In many ways this book could be compared to a gourmet meal, a culinary delight, prepared by a fine chef. I hear Vincent's a very fine chef. He claims to be an even better chef than he is a photographer. (!)

This may hurt, but you'll enjoy the ride. Here's Vincent's teaching style in a nutshell. "I'll throw you in the water. I'll throw you a life preserver. I'll be in the boat next to you. But you're swimming. The only way to learn is total immersion."

Way beyond technique (though you'll get plenty of that too), this is a book on perception. Read it and you'll see differently. Read it and you'll find yourself immersed in sensuous pools of color. Read it and you'll fan the flames of your love of light. Read it and you'll find your experience of the elasticity of time intensified. Read it.

This book will make you think. This book will make you feel. This book will make you respond.

Scream.

Scream in fear. At first absorbing this material seems overwhelmingly complex. Have faith in yourself. A mountain is climbed one step at a time. Break this challenge down into pieces, tackle each piece one at a time, then put it all back together again—in your own way.

Scream in amazement. The medium of photography is no longer what you thought it was. Perhaps it never was. But then, who can pin down this fast-evolving chimera?

Scream for joy. You now have more technical power and creative freedom than you have ever had before.

Vincent believes in you. He believes "the next Michelangelo is a soccer mom." And he's not about to underestimate your intelligence.

Vincent knows being here is what it's all about.

These are Vincent's words. "Here's hope. You may not know how to get there, but you can get there. Walk with me."

Creativity is addictive.

—John Paul Caponigro

Introduction

Sometimes you read a book and you understand it, and sometimes you read a book and it understands you.

—Bjork

In the past, when I bought "how-to" books, I bought them by weight. The equation was a simple one: I assumed that the heavier the book, the more knowledge it contained. Over the years I accumulated lots of answers, I just didn't know any of the questions. I had the *how*, but no idea of the *why*. What I have discovered is that the *why* is more important than the *how*. If you know what you want to do and why you want to do it, discovering how becomes mere detail.

This book is not intended to teach you how Photoshop works, nor does it offer a "12-steps-to-perfect-photos," one-size-fits-all workflow. Rather, this book is about engaging in a conversation that will lead to teaching yourself to be able to make magic, starting at the point of capture. There is a circularness to photography. Because you are in service of the print (the end) which is your voice, the more you know about image editing (the middle), the more informed your decisions can be when you make your captures (the beginning). We will be traveling in a circle, but we will be doing it in a straight line.

This is a book about exploring how to express your vision. No one can teach you how to become an artist. Art, and being called an artist, are social terms. You don't create art by deciding that's what you are going to do today, and you don't become an artist by proclaiming yourself as one. In my eyes, nothing I do is art. For me, it's expression. It becomes art when other people call it so. In the moment that "art" happens for the viewer of my work, I am an artist.

It is of ultimate importance that you create only those images that you find worthy. Others cannot like what you do not. I know that my harshest critic sits in the same chair I do. I offer you this thought—there are enough people in the world who want to beat you up; don't help them. Create images that please you. If you think you have an image with unfulfilled potential, don't discard it as worthless. Determine what about the image should be different and then transform it so it becomes an expression of your voice.

The experience that this book is designed to create is one that mimics, as closely as possible, the real-world experience of image editing. To this end, included with this book, you have received full-resolution, 16-bit source files (not 72-dot-per-inch low-resolution work files) on which to work. In case the computer with which you are working has less horsepower than you would like, there is also an 8-bit set of source files. Additionally, there is a 100-ppi version of the source file that was created during the writing of each chapter's lesson, so that you can see what these files look like in your environment, that is, on your calibrated monitor on your computer.

There is one basic assumption that I made when I wrote this book. I assumed that you are working on a monitor that is calibrated with a hardware-based monitor calibration device, like a GretagMacbeth Eye-One device or the Monaco XBR. Other than that, I assume nothing other than that you believe that the journey is the destination.

What digital photography has shown me is that impossible is just an opinion. For the first time in my creative life, I can realize my vision and express it for others to see. This is the journey on which I wish to take you. It is the reason that I wrote this book.

The Core Concepts of a Cinematic Approach to Digital Still Photography

Though this book's entire focus is on the why and how of developing a cinematic approach to digital still photography with Photoshop, what follows are the core concepts that are the foundation of this approach.

Photoshop is not a verb. It is a noun. It is the means to an end, not the end itself. Photoshop is not the reason you take a picture, it is a tool to help you realize your vision. Photoshop, though one of the most inspired pieces of software ever written, was not meant to be used as a jackhammer; it was intended to be used as an emery board. Should you ever be asked whether or not you altered an image in Photoshop, you want it to be a question, not an accusation.

A still photograph is called a still photograph because the picture doesn't move, not because the objects in the picture are not in motion. This is the single most important consideration when taking a photograph. What occurs in a properly executed still photograph is that motion is captured with stillness. If we were to take a 35mm movie camera, place a flower that was just beginning to bud in front of it, let the movie camera fire off one frame a minute for two weeks while the flower blossomed, develop the film, and play what we shot at 28 frames per second, we would see the flower open up before our eyes and then the petals drop off. At no time did the flower stop moving; what was stopped was the motion of the flower. Things happen at the speed of life. They do not happen at one frame a second or even 8.5 or 28 frames a second.

"RGB is not a color. RGB is a formula to mix color." If you can see it with your eye, it's a color. How you control color is one of the elements that will determine how the viewer's eye moves across a print. From the moment of capture, understanding the formula to mix color will make your images more successful when they are printed.

NOTE: This core concept was originally taught to me by Eric Magnusson, and it is one that we will revisit a number of times in this book.

There are two "eyes" that view an image, the unconscious eye and the conscious eye. The unconscious eye is an optical organic device that "sees" in a predictable manner. By controlling how the unconscious eye moves across an image, you can determine the story that the conscious eye perceives.

If something you see moves you, take a picture of it. Do not hesitate. If you hesitate, the moment is lost. The moments of life happen, they don't re-happen. Viola Spolin said, "In absolute spontaneity, you get absolute truth. You can only be one way when you are spontaneous, and that's truthful." By staying in the moment and allowing the spontaneity of your experience to cause the shutter to be fired, all of your images will have in them the truth of what you felt and saw. If you preconceive what you are going to shoot, the images lose that truth, that reality.

Visualize the finished image in your mind's eye as you are taking the picture and not a moment before. You do this so that when you get to the image editing process, you already have the end in mind. When you approach shooting images this way, you can remove everything that is not your vision. But even though you want to hold a clear vision of what you want the image to be, don't start with preconceptions about what you are going to shoot. Walk into the taking of pictures open to what is out there, without any preconceptions.

Get it right in the camera. If it doesn't look good through the lens, it will not look good coming out of the printer. Even if you find yourself in a situation that does not allow you to make the captures as you would have liked, get as much right in camera as you can. Make informed decisions as you shoot, keeping in mind what images you might need when you get to image editing in Photoshop, so that your choices are not compromises.

Compose your images, don't crop them. Cinematographers do not have the luxury of cropping an image in the darkroom or the computer. What they see in the viewfinder is the canvas on which they have to paint. You are responsible for every millimeter of every image frame you create. Fill it! Place your subject in places other than the center of the frame. Bulls-eye composition is great if you are a marksman, but in the creation of a photograph, it is generally not considered to be a preferable style choice.

Workflow starts at the point of capturing the image and is dynamic, not static. No two images are the same, therefore no two workflows are the same. Be adaptive. Always pro-act, don't react. Be willing to improvise, and you will find the impossible within your reach.

In the ensuing chapters, just a few of the subjects we will explore are: light, gesture, shape, time, color, and the formula to mix color. It is my hope that when you arrive at the last word of the last chapter in this book, you will have attained the same skill set as I have. Your vision is not limited by your skills—only by your imagination. Your skills help you to communicate your vision to others. With that said, we begin.

FIGURE 1.1 *Before.*

FIGURE 1.2 *The final result.*

Chapter 1

The Tao of Dynamic Workflow

Practice doesn't make perfect. Perfect practice makes perfect.
You first have to practice at practicing.

—Vince Lombardi

This chapter deals with how to analyze an image and develop a dynamic, image-specific workflow, so that you can achieve in the print the image as you conceptualized it. I will place special focus on image mapping and how to do basic lighting in Photoshop. I will also take a broader look at how to approach images and think about them. This lesson is about learning how to practice at practicing and then about how to find the path to perfect practice.

Shibumi:
The Art of Perfect Practice

The image in this chapter is a picture of the actress Challen Cates from a photo shoot I did in Los Angeles using a single piece of lighting gear, a 6' × 3' diffuser. The reason only a diffuser was used to light this image is that when I arrived at the location, the lighting equipment had not. As a result, all I had was the diffuser that I had loaded, as an afterthought, into my assistant's car. Once on location, I could either *react* to the situation and call it a day, or I could be proactive and *adapt* and *improvise*; i.e., go ahead with the shoot believing that "impossible" is just an opinion and that by adapting and improvising I would be able to achieve my original purpose. Choosing to be proactive, I had my assistant hold the diffuser over Challen's head so that she was evenly lit. I knew that if she was evenly lit, I would have the best possible source file with which to work so I could later "light" her properly in the computer.

NOTE: Every image in this book marks a significant milestone in the development of my approach to creating images. Each represents a moment of discovery—an epiphany—in which I found a new way to create, in print, what my eye had initially determined should be there.

I truly believe that it is best to approach Photoshop preemptively, to *get it right in the camera,* and that Photoshop is best used as an emery board and not a jackhammer. If it doesn't look good when viewing it through the camera, it will not look good coming out of the printer. Even when the situation doesn't lend itself to getting it perfect, as in the case of the Challen Cates shoot, at the time of capture you should get as much right as possible.

In order to know how to *get it right in the camera*, which is the beginning of the process, you must understand the middle and end of the process as well. The middle of the process is *the manipulation of the file in Photoshop* and its end is *the print*, which is your voice, your vision.

To reiterate, this lesson will teach you how to analyze an image and develop a dynamic, image-specific workflow, so that you can achieve in the print the image as you conceptualized it. You will be able to do this because you will gain an understanding of maximizing capture, so that manipulation of the file in Photoshop will result in the print you wanted to achieve. Because of the circumstances of the Challen Cates shoot, the image that I had in my head when I captured it was nothing like the image I was forced to take—an image with almost no variation in light, dark, contrast, saturation, focus, or blur. I knew, however, that if I kept my initial vision in my head, using Photoshop I could create those variations within that picture, so that it would be transformed into what I knew it should become.

The Secret of Dynamic Workflow

There is no such thing as a workflow recipe, no promise that "if you follow these simple steps, you will always have great work." No two images are the same and no two images will ever require the same workflow. Some images are just easier than others to work with, and you may not know before you begin into which category any single image will fall.

To achieve a truly organized workflow, you must be adaptable and open to improvisation. It is through such improvisation that you overcome obstacles. But it is by practicing at practicing that you can find the way to engage in perfect practice. So how do you achieve perfect practice? Perfect practice occurs when you unconsciously, and without effort, adapt and improvise in order to overcome obstacles. The Japanese call it "being in *Shibumi*." This lesson is about learning how to be in Shibumi whenever and wherever you create.

Practicing at Practicing: Image Maps

Step 1: Using Image Maps

As an optical sensing device, the human eye scans a scene in a predictable sequence. It first goes to patterns it recognizes, then moves from areas of light to dark, high contrast to low contrast, high sharpness to low sharpness, in focus to blur (which is different than high to low sharpness), and high saturation to low saturation of color.

In order to make the viewer's eye move across the image in a way that you decide it should, so that the image can be seen in the same way you did, you must manipulate the light and dark areas, their contrast, their sharpness, their degree of focus or blur, and their saturation.

Controlling the variables just mentioned may appear to be a daunting task making you feel overwhelmed by the amount of work to be done. The best way to start is by creating a list of the changes you would like to make. How best to do this is by creating an image map.

An *image map* is a Photoshop layer that sits on top of the image layer stack, on which you can make notes and lists of what you are planning to do to an image. You can also use it to make notations on the various steps you will take, but what it does best is teach you how to create image-specific work-flows. An image map is basically a planning device that helps you see the trees from the forest.

NOTE: Keep in mind that image maps are designed to go away. They are the equivalent of training wheels. They are a good way to teach yourself how to organize and see, but you won't need them forever. To practice at practicing, you should do every lesson in this book with them and again without them.

Also, although it is possible to do everything in all the lessons in this book with a mouse or even the trackpad of a laptop, you will be better served if you use a pen- or tablet-based system.

Before I give you the first "how to" step toward creating an image map, consider how "believable" you would like the finished image to appear. In this lesson, you do not want the viewer to know that you did any manipulation in Photoshop; you want to create an imitation of what would have occurred had the model been properly lit in the first place.

A way to explain this can be found in Aristotle's, *The Poetics*. In this work, he suggested that a believable improbability is better than an improbable believability. I believe this to be true and have extended this concept to define believable probability. What are these concepts and why are they important to digital photography?

The easiest way to understand these concepts is by using examples. Good examples of *believable improbability* are found in the Star Wars sagas. We don't travel faster than the speed of light, and walking, talking robots with feelings don't yet exist. In spite of this, we are willing to suspend disbelief, because the stories of love, longing, and conflict ring true or are *believable* even though they are *improbable*. In contrast, what follows is an example of *improbable believability*. I buy a lottery ticket in Los Angeles on my way back from the airport. The drawing is that night and the jackpot is $100,000.00. I win!! The next day, I fly to New York City and buy another ticket. The jackpot is $75,000,000.00. I win again!!! The next day I fly to Chicago and I figure, "Why not?" I buy another lottery ticket and I win again!!! Although this could happen, you don't believe it because it is so *improbable*.

The third concept, that of *believable probability*, can be explained using the Challen Cates image. What we will do is to create an image using Photoshop that the viewer will find both probable and believable, because the final image will be lit as though we had had the proper lighting equipment when we made the initial image capture.

In order to assure that we create a *believable probability* rather than an *improbable believability*, we need to make sure that every choice we make in Photoshop leads to a result that will mimic the reality of proper lighting. For example, if we create a light that appears to shine from above, we need to create corresponding shadows that follow the direction of that light.

There will be images in which you will want to create a *believable improbability*. (There are some in this book. Try to identify them as you progress through the lessons.) The key to making something believable, no matter how improbable it may be, is to make sure that it conforms to the logic of our reality as much as possible. Once you've defined your goal for any particular image, you can begin to create your image maps.

Creating an Image Map

1. Open the image SHIBUMI SOURCE.tif (located in the CHAPTER 1 folder) in Photoshop and make sure the image is in the neutral gray workspace by pressing the letter F. The gray space is best for making color decisions.

NOTE: There are two sets of source files for you to use on the disc that accompanies this book. There is a set of 16-bit files, and in case your computer does not have the ability to handle those, a set of 8-bit source files as well. All the instructions, as well as all the lessons, will call for the 16-bit files.

Using gray gives you an uncluttered and color-neutral background. Gray is specifically used to minimize chromatic induction (visual color contamination). A mid-tone (gray) is used to minimize contrast effects. By choosing a gray background,

you can make the most informed and accurate decisions about how to change the color, contrast, and shade of the image with which you're working.

2. View the image in full screen (Ctrl-0/Cmd-0), choose the Pencil tool, and double click on the "set foreground color" box in the Tools palette (the black and white squares located toward the bottom of the Tools palette). This brings up the color picker dialogue box. Select a bright color. (I generally choose red and then work my way down on the color selector.)

3. Make sure the Layers palette is open and click the New Layer button. Call the new layer L2D IM (for Light to Dark Image Map).

NOTE: At any level of expertise, giving your layers meaningful file names is an important part of creating an effective workflow. If many months after working on a file, you want to return to it to try a new technique, you will immediately grasp the purpose of each layer on which you originally worked and be able to retrieve the appropriate one on which to try your new approach. Or suppose you made a print or sent a file to a client, and changes are needed. Knowing at a glance what you did to the image will make life a lot easier should you have to go back and redo or undo something. It also makes your practicing at practicing sessions easier. If you get lost, you have an easily readable and retrievable road map.

4. Select a brush size of 30 pixels. (You increase or diminish a brush's size by pressing the square bracket keys, which are on the keyboard next to the letter P. Pressing the left bracket makes the brush smaller; pressing the right bracket makes it bigger.)

NOTE: Correct brush size is determined by the size and resolution of the image, so focus on the visual size of the brush, and not on its pixel size. For example, a 30-pixel brush would be much too large to use on a small, low-resolution image.

The Relationship of Light to Dark

For this lesson, we will manipulate only two of the variables that I mentioned at the beginning of Step 1: light-to-dark and in-focus-to-blur. Remember, it is the person creating the image who decides the journey that the viewer's eye will take. And it is that journey that causes the viewer to see the story you wanted to tell.

How we control where the viewer's eye will go is by manipulating variables such as focus, and light and dark. I contend that when we view anything at all, there is both an unconscious and a conscious element involved. First, our unconscious eye, or the anatomic structure that makes up the eye, scans in the predictable manner I described above. Then, the conscious eye, the mind's eye, interprets the image seen by the unconscious eye. It is how we control the unconscious eye that determines how the viewer interprets the image. This is a theme to which I will frequently return.

In general, I like to begin manipulating light-to-dark, thereby exploiting the unconscious eye's tendency to move from light areas to dark ones. For this specific image, I want the viewer's eye to go first to the face, then to the torso, then to the rest of the image.

You must first decide what ratio or relationship of light-to-dark to create within this image. I wanted the face to be brightest, so I set it at 100%. As light's circle of illumination increases, its intensity diminishes, so set the hair and torso at 50%. The background should be darker than the face, hair, and torso. The light on the background should go from light to dark as the eye moves from right to left. (I'll explain why in a moment.) Set the right side at 25% and the left side at 0%.

NOTE: As you create your image map, keep in mind that these percentages are just notations. You can change them any time. At this point, we are making broad strokes. We will refine them later. I always suggest working from the global to the granular.

After those values are drawn on the L2D IM layer, the image will look like this (**Figure 1.3**):

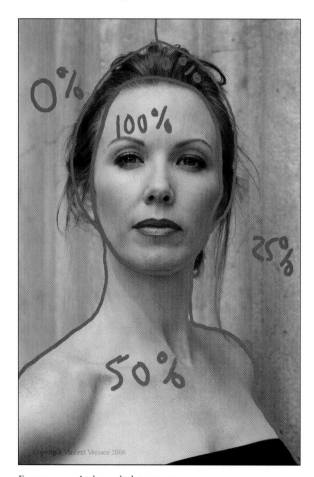

FIGURE 1.3 *Light-to-dark image map.*

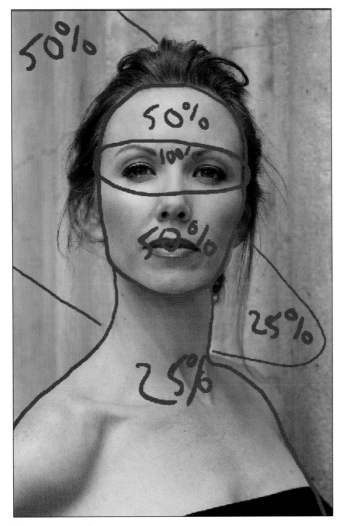

FIGURE 1.4 *Lighting image map.*

Placing Key and Fill Lights

If I had had all my lighting equipment at the photo shoot, I would have started by lighting the background, and I would have cross-lit it from left to right. Then I would have set key lights and fill lights. With a portrait, you usually want the viewer's eye to go first to the subject's eyes, so that's where you should put the key light. Then you might put fill lights on the lips and to some degree, the torso.

Create a new layer and name it LIGHTING IM (for Lighting Image Map). Pick a color other than red from the Tools palette to draw your lighting choices. (I chose blue.)

Here is the LIGHTING image map (**Figure 1.4**) showing the notation of the percentages used: eyes 100%, face 50%, torso 25%, and background areas 50% and 25%.

The Illusion of Depth of Field

When shooting portraits, I find that a shallow depth of field, where the background is out of focus and only the subject is sharp, is visually pleasing. When you focus on the subject's eye that is closest to the camera, the depth of field (the zone of acceptable sharpness) on the face will extend from the tip of the nose to a little past the ear. Generally that means shooting at f/5.6.

Create a new layer and name it D OF F (for Depth of Field), and pick a new color to use for your next set of image map notations. (I chose light green.)

In this case, the image was shot at f/6.3, with the model standing right against the wall, underneath the diffuser. The result? Too much depth of field, with everything in focus, including the background.

Depth of field refers to the area that is in focus both in front and behind the true point of focus. It has been shown that if the depth of the area that appears to be in focus in front of the true point of focus is 1 foot, then the area that appears to be in focus behind the true point of focus is 2 feet. This works out to a ratio of one-third in front in focus to two-thirds behind in focus; i.e. twice as much behind as in front.

The absolute distance that is in focus depends on two factors: the size of the lens aperture and the distance from the camera to the subject. The larger the aperture, the "shallower" or smaller the area that is in focus. The smaller the aperture, the "deeper" or greater the area that is in focus. Additionally, the farther away a subject becomes from the camera, the greater its depth of field, i.e. the more that will be in focus. Conversely, the closer the subject is to the camera, the less its depth of field, i.e. the less that will be in focus.

Many photographers have the mistaken belief that shorter focal length lenses have a greater depth of field than do longer focal length lenses. We can illustrate why this misunderstanding exists with the following example. If we set up a tripod, and compose and shoot a scene using a 200mm lens, and then change to a 35mm lens at the same position without changing the aperture, the 35mm frame will appear to have a greater depth of field. This occurs, however, only because the 35mm lens has a much larger field of view. To accurately compare the depth of field of the 200mm lens to the 35mm lens, we must move in with the 35mm lens until the field of view exactly matches the field of view we had with the 200mm lens at the original position. When the resulting images

are compared, the depth of field for the two lenses will be exactly the same.

In the lighting image map, we made some decisions as to where we would like the viewer's eye to go: first to the face, then the torso, and then the background from right to left. The face and torso are easy to understand, but why right to left? Because we want to create the illusion that the model is farther from the background than she really is. With that in mind, you will sweep from left to right from 75% to 25%, leave the face at 100%, and set the torso at 10% (**Figure 1.5**).

Figure 1.5

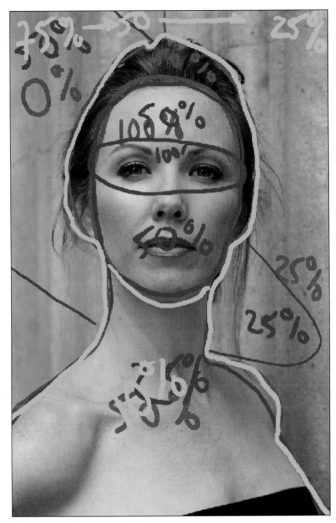

FIGURE 1.6 *A composite of the image maps used up to now.*

NOTE: One of the issues that occurred during Challen's photo shoot was that in order to evenly light her, I had to place her almost against the wall. I would have preferred that she be some distance away from and at an angle to the wall. In order to create this illusion in Photoshop so as to achieve a believable probability, we have to create the correct quantity of in-focus-to-blur that would have occurred had we actually lit her properly and positioned her away from the wall. We also need to apply some degree of blur to her torso. (Since the point of focus is her eye, and one-third forward from that point should be focus, the area in focus should stop at the tip of her nose. Any areas of her torso that extend past her nose should not be in focus.)

You now have a basic workflow to follow for manipulating the lighting and depth of field of the Challen Cates image in Photoshop (**Figure 1.6**). (Keep in mind that the values I chose to use are only approximations, and reflect relationships specific to this image.) You are now well on the way to a believable probability, the original vision of the image, from a completely flat-lit photograph.

Make the image maps invisible. They will be out of the way, but available when needed.

Step 2: Correcting Digital Sensor Color Cast

Now that you have an image roadmap, working from global to granular, let's address the next biggest issue, correcting the image's CCD/CMOS color cast. It is an important issue because it will affect all of the image editing choices you will make from this point on.

All RAW images, from any digital camera, exhibit a color cast as a result of the interpolation process that occurs when you bring that image into digital manipulation software such as Photoshop. The Challen Cates image has a magenta/yellow haze.

The most effective way that I have found to remove this type of color cast is to first define the black and white points of the image on which you are working. Finding the white point is a bit more problematic than finding the black point, but you are going to find them both by using a Threshold adjustment layer.

NOTE: Something to keep in mind is that Threshold does not use absolute RGB values in equal amounts, but combines them using the standard formula: roughly ~60% green, ~30% red, and ~10% blue. This means that measurable white and visible white are often two very different things, something you will understand as we go through the steps of color cast correction.

There are some rules that are important to know when removing the color cast caused from the interpolation of the data from a CCD/CMOS sensor. First, when looking for the black point, select your sample point from an area of "meaningful" black rather than using the first black pixel you see. If you select the very first black pixel that you see, it generally has RGB values that are R:0, B:0, G:0. If no information was recorded, no color contamination exists. What we are looking for is a black pixel that has RGB information in it.

Finding a white point is completely different. You do not want to select a white point from an area of "meaningful" white. Rather, you want to find the pixels that are closest to pure white, without actually being pure white. (A pure white pixel will have RGB values of R:255, G:255, B:255, which is of the same usefulness as a black pixel that has RGB values that are zero.) What makes finding a white point so problematic is that, much of the time, visible white and measurable white are two different things. (Measurable white, using the Threshold adjustment layer method, will always be biased to 60%G, 30%R, 10% B. Visible white generally consists of equal values of RGB and tends to be a lot bluer than measurable white.) In addition, there are instances when there is no "white point" and occasionally there may be aspects of the white point color

cast correction you may not like, i.e. you may actually like aspects of the color cast. For these reasons, it's a good idea to separate the black and white points into two curves adjustment layers; it gives you options.

NOTE: Looking at this image, visible white is found in the catch light of the subject's eye.

How To Find Black and White Points Using a Threshold Adjustment Layer

1. Make the background layer active. Go to the bottom of the Layers palette and create a Threshold adjustment layer. (Go to the bottom of the layers pallet, click on the "Create a Fill or Adjustment Layer" icon and select Threshold.) A black-and-white representation of the image appears (**Figure 1.7a**).

Figure 1.7a

FIGURE 1.7B

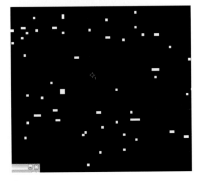

FIGURES 1.7C AND 1.7D

2. Move the triangle slider (located at the bottom of the threshold dialog) to the left until the image goes completely white. As you move the slider slowly back toward the right, you will see image detail start to emerge in black. The first meaningful area of black that you see is where you will take your black sample point (**Figure 1.7b**). (Meaningful black is an area in which we can see "something.")

Choose a black point from the top of the model's dress. You do this by zooming into this area of the dress (Ctrl+Space/ Command+Space to give you the Zoom tool) and then Shift clicking a sample point (**Figures 1.7c** and **1.7d**).

NOTE: Looking at this image, even though we see "meaningful" black in the hair and eye areas, I chose to put my black point down in the model's dress because her dress was actually black. You will notice, however, that the dress's color recorded as dark blue.

3. Now bring the image back to full screen (Ctrl-0/Cmd-0), and move the triangle slider all the way to the right. The image will be completely black, but you should see a sample point in the lower right corner with the number "1." That's your black point.

4. Move the slider slowly back to the left until the first area of white pixels appear.

NOTE: Remember, when it comes to choosing a potential white point, get as close to the first white pixel that you see as you can. If that pixel has an RGB value of R:255, G:255, B:255, then get as close as you can to the first white pixel without actually selecting it.

The two areas that come up are on the shoulder and somewhere on the face. Zoom into each area and shift click to select a sample point. One of these is the image's potential white point.

5. Click "cancel" on the Threshold dialog. It's only needed to help you locate the potential white and black points.

The image appears in color again, but now displays three sample points: one on the model's forehead, one on her shoulder, and one on her dress. The series of numbers that appear in the Info palette are the actual color values of the sample points. (Sample point 1(BP): R=21, B=23, G=41. Sample point 2 (WP 2): R=250, B=251, G=191. Sample Point 3 (WP 3): R=254, G=254, B=252.)

NOTE: If your numbers don't exactly match mine, it only means that we picked slightly different sample points. Notice that neither of the areas you clicked on for your white point was located in the area of the eye. In this instance, visible white is different from measurable white. For the purpose of demonstration, I placed a white sample point (and named it Sample Point 4) in the specular highlight of the eye. This is the whitest visible white point in the image.

6. Turn Caps Lock on; the pointer becomes the crosshairs cursor. Go to the bottom of the Layers palette, and click on the "Create new fill or adjustment layer" radial button. (It is the third radial button from the left. It is a circle that is half white and half black.) Select "Curves" from the fly-out menu. We are now going to create the first of two Curves adjustment layers.

7. When the Curves dialog box comes up, click the black eyedropper. Now, double-click on the black eyedropper that is located in the lower right corner of the dialog box. The Color Picker dialog box will come up. In the RGB values part of the dialog box, type 7 in the R, 7 in the G, and 7 in the B. Click OK (**Figure 1.7e**).

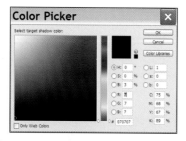

FIGURE 1.7E

Adjustment Layers vs. Image > Adjustment Commands

If you use the Image > Adjustment commands approach to editing your images, you are making permanent changes to the pixels on the active layer. On the other hand, an adjustment layer is a layer of math that sits above the layer stack and, though it effects the image the same way as using an Image > Adjustment command, it does not make permanent changes to the pixels of the active layer.

It's a better idea to use adjustment layers rather than adjustment commands because:

1. An adjustment layer can later be re-opened and the settings changed by double-clicking the left-hand thumbnail.
2. An adjustment layer can be hidden to temporarily remove its effect or it can be deleted to permanently remove the adjustment.
3. When using a layer mask, an adjustment layer can be selectively applied to various parts of the image.
4. An adjustment layer can be used to apply an adjustment to all of the layers below it in the Layers palette.
5. An adjustment layer can be "clipped" to a single layer by Option-clicking/Alt-clicking on the line in the Layers palette between the adjustment layer and the layer immediately below. This restricts the adjustment to the single layer.
6. An adjustment layer can be applied to some, but not all, of the layers in the Layers palette. To do this, add the layers to which you want to apply the adjustment to a layer Group, place the adjustment layer within the Group at the top, and change the Group's blending mode from Pass Through to Normal.

NOTE: The RGB values of R:7 B:7 G:7 approximate the beginning of what is known as Zone II (textured black) in the Zone system, as developed by Ansel Adams and Minor White. For further discussion of the Zone System, see *The Zone System* by Minor White.

When you define the white point, you will set the white point eyedropper for the upper end of Zone IX (textured white). The reason for this is that, in a fine art print, you are looking for 100% ink coverage in the highlights (no place where the paper shows through the ink) and shadows that have detail throughout. In other words, we want no paper showing and no ink wasted.

Zoom into the area of sample point 1. You should see a circle with two crosshairs. Select the black eyedropper, which is the leftmost eyedropper of the three in the Curves adjustment layer dialogue box. Line the two crosshairs up until it appears that there is only one, and click. Notice how the color changes. Click OK.

Blending Modes

Blending modes are algorithms assigned to layers (or tools) which affect how they interact with other layers. The blending mode assigned to a layer (the "blend" color layer) determines how the colors of the pixels on that layer interact with the colors of the pixels on the base color layer or layers below. The result of that interaction is know as the "result color." When working with tools, the blending mode of the tool affects how that tool will alter the pixels on every layer below (their color, transparency, saturation, etc.).

NOTE: Photoshop will ask if you, "Want to save the new target colors as default?" Click "yes" for both the black and white point curves.

Also, as I discussed in the introduction of this book, RGB is not a color, it's a formula to mix color. What you are doing here is addressing issues of color, specifically color cast. For that reason, you are going to leave the blending mode of this Curves adjustment layer, as well as the one you are about to create, as "Normal."

8. In the Layers palette, name this layer BP (for Black Point). By redefining the black point, you have also removed the CCD/CMOS color cast from the black parts of the image (**Figures 1.7f** and **1.7g**).

FIGURE 1.7F *Before.*

FIGURE 1.7G *After.*

9. Bring the image back to full screen. Repeat the steps for creating a Curves adjustment layer. Select the Set White Point eyedropper. Double click on the White Eyedropper and set the RGB values to R:247, G:247 and B:247. (This approximates the upper end of Zone IX.) Click OK. Zoom into the area of Sample point 2, align the cross hairs, click, and then click OK. You have set the white point. The color cast disappears (**Figure 1.7h**).

NOTE: In the file SHIBUMI16 BIT 100PPI.psd, I have placed sample points on the shoulder, the forehead, and the white highlight in the eye. I have also created Curves adjustment layers for each of the sample points. Take a look at what all three look like. To my eye, WP2 looks best. Notice that if you zoom in to the area of sample point 4, even though this area appears to be the whitest, it is also the bluest. As we discussed, the Threshold adjustment layer we used measured 60% Red, 30% Green, and 10% Blue. That is why the visible white of this image is bluer than its measurable white, which will appear redder/greener.

FIGURE 1.7H *The color cast is now gone.*

You have successfully removed the CCD/CMOS color cast from the "white" aspects of the image, thereby eliminating the color contamination inherent in the process of converting RAW files to any usable file format.

Step 3: Merging Layers in "The Move"

You will now merge copies of the layers you've created so far into a single new layer, while preserving the individual work layers that you created earlier. Adobe Photoshop refers to this as Merge Stamp Visible. I prefer to refer to this as doing "The Move." Note that you are merging the layers into one without flattening the image. This is an important distinction because if you just merge layers, you also flatten the resultant image thereby losing all the original layers. If you do this, you will have no exit strategy, no way to return to the image, and you will be unable to practice at practicing.

Make sure you are at the top of the layer heap by making the topmost visible layer active. For CS2 and above, press and hold Ctrl-Alt-Shift-E/Cmd-Option-Shift-E. For CS and below, press Ctrl-Alt-Shift/Cmd-Option-Shift, then type N, and then E.

You now have a base image layer on which you can start to work to make other aesthetically pleasing changes. Name it MASTER 1. "Save As" the file (Shft+Ctrl+S/ Shft+Command+S) and name the file SHIBUMI 16BIT and save the image as a Photoshop document (.psd).

NOTE: I have a system for saving and naming files. I always save the layered files with which I'm working as Photoshop documents (.PSD). I save all of the files that I use for printing as Tiff files (.TIF), but I do not save layered Tiffs. Not all programs that can open Tiffs can read layered Tiffs, and sometimes layered Tiffs can cause programs that can't read them to crash. Also, Windows OS has a peccadillo; it does not show thumbnails of layered files. It also does not show thumbnails of any file on the desktop, except for Genuine Fractal files (.STN). Because I will eventually scale all of my files, I save them as Genuine Fractal lossless files. Once they are scaled, I save the scaled file as a Genuine Fractal visually lossless file.

So that I can recognize how I saved a file, I add 16 Bit or 8 Bit to the filename. For Tiffs, I add the canvas size. For example, SHIBUMII 13x19.TIF would mean that its canvas size is 13 inches by 19 inches. SHIBUMI 24x30 VL.STN would mean that the canvas is 24 × 30 inches and that it is a Genuine Fractal visually lossless file. *Always* give your layers and files meaningful names and *always* give yourself an exit strategy as you develop your personal approach to workflow.

NOTE: If you are using a pen-based workflow either with a graphics tablet or pen display like a Cintiq, or a device like the Logitec NuLOOQ navigator tool dial, you can program this set of keystrokes into the pop-up menu on the Cintiq or NuLOOQ tool dial menu. Then just click a button and voilà—"The Move" will happen.

Step 4: Correcting for the Blue Color Cast of Sunlight

Wherever possible, I try to come up with the "Photoshop" way of doing things, and most of the time I succeed. But what makes Photoshop such a unique software package is that Adobe designed a way for us to use add-ons (called plug-ins) without messing with the core of the program. Some things can be done more easily or elegantly with third-party technology.

In my pursuit of a smoother workflow, I have become an advocate of the filters made by Nik Multimedia. For example, if you aren't using their Skylight filter, I think you should.

NOTE: You can download free versions of the Nik Skylight and Contrast filters at: www.niksoftware.com/ozlessons.

A skylight filter can correct for the fact that shade and shadow light tends to be bluer than direct light, and direct light tends to be bluer than early morning and late afternoon light. The filter scans the image and determines how much, and where, red needs to be added to counteract any blue cast.

1. Duplicate the MASTER 1 layer and rename the copy SKYLIGHT

NOTE: A quick way to duplicate a layer is to use the keyboard command Control+J for windows or Command+J for Apple. Although this is the keyboard command for duplicating a selection, you can also use it to duplicate a layer.

2. Choose Filter > Nik Color Efex Pro 2.0: traditional filters > Skylight Filter.

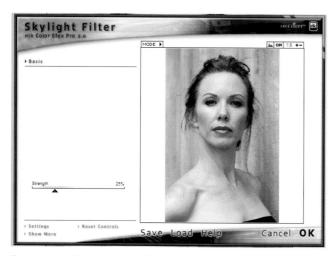

FIGURE 1.8 *The Nik Skylight Filter interface.*

FIGURE 1.9 *Before using the Skylight filter.*

FIGURE 1.10 *After Skylight color correction.*

The Skylight Filter menu appears. The default setting (25%) is fine for our purposes, so click OK (**Figure 1.8**).

First and foremost, you want to make sure that you are creating a believable probability. In the real world, shadows tend to be bluer or "cooler" than areas that are well lit. Areas that are "lit" tend to be "warmer" (red/yellow) than areas that are not. People look better "warmer" than "cooler." Knowing this, what you want to do is create selective warmth in the image so that it follows the roadmap that you defined in your initial image maps (L 2 d L2D IM and LIGHTING IM layers). You will accomplish this is by using a layer mask (**Figures 1.9** and **1.10**).

3. To selectively apply the Skylight filter effect, use a layer mask. To create a layer mask, go to the bottom of the layers palette. Holding down the Alt/Option key, click on the "Add Layer Mask" radio button. (This is the third radio button from the left.) This is the one-click way to create a layer mask and fill it with black.

4. Make the L2D IM and LIGHTING IM layers visible so that you can analyze how to selectively warm this image (**Figures 1.11a** and **1.11b**).

5. Choose a very soft brush, roughly the size of the eye socket. Start with an opacity of 50% (press the number 5 key), and make sure the foreground color is white.

NOTE: The keyboard command to change a brush's opacity is simple. Just type in the number value of the opacity percentage you want: 0=100%, 5=50%, 2=20%, 1=10% and so on.

You now face a conceptually tricky task. Because you are working with a layer mask filled with black, but painting with white, you are dealing with a negative image as you would in a black-and-white darkroom. Therefore, you are working in reverse.

FIGURE 1.11A *Image before painting in warm tones.*

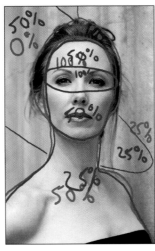

FIGURE 1.11B *Image with image map before painting in the warm tones.*

FIGURE 1.12A *After the tones have been selectively painted in.*

FIGURE 1.12B *The layer mask.*

You are going to be building up different levels of intensity of warmth (the "warmth" that you have just created using the Skylight filter), and since you want the eyes to be brightest, start by brushing that area at 50%. (Remember, all brushwork is cumulative.)

When you're done, this is the area you will want to be the warmest in the image. For the first part of the lesson, paint inside the lines on the image map. Don't worry about being exact; just use the lines as an approximation (**Figure 1.12a**).

The layer mask now has a whitish streak across it. This is the area you are revealing. Next, re-brush over the face at 50% twice so that the eyes will be at 100% opacity and the face at 75% (**Figure 1.12b**).

6. Select an opacity of 20%, increase the brush size one step by pressing the right bracket (]) key, and paint in the torso. Shrink the brush three sizes by pressing the left bracket ([) key three times, and brush in the hair. Now increase the opacity to 50%, increase the brush size four times, and brush the face and the area behind the subject.

7. Lastly, reduce the brush four sizes and paint the area in which background light should fall off, as you originally mapped it on the image maps.

Layer masks are a powerful Photoshop tool and an important way to control the aesthetics of an image. A layer mask works by allowing you to hide or reveal (either completely or partially) filter effects, adjustment layer corrections, or anything you want to selectively control.

The best way to remember how to work on a layer mask is by remembering this simple mnemonic: "Black conceals and white reveals." That means that black will block the visibility of the effect you are creating, whereas white will allow the effect to be visible.

A good way to ensure an efficient work flow is to use what is referred to as the "80/20 rule." If you want to reveal 80% and conceal 20% of the layer, create a white mask and paint with black to conceal. If you want to conceal 80% and reveal 20% of the layer, start with a black mask and paint the areas you want to reveal with white.

Since you are working in grayscale when you are working on a layer mask, varying levels of black or white opacity determines how much or how little of the effect on that layer you allow to be seen. In other words, if you are working on a white layer mask, the darker the gray, the less that is revealed, and when you are working on a black layer mask, the lighter the gray, the more that is revealed.

0521 Rule

I have found that there is a relationship between 100%, 50%, 25% and 10% opacity. The 0521 rule is based on this observation. The way the rule works is this: 50% of 50% is 25%. So if you're working at 50% opacity, and you want to increase the effect of the thing on which you're working, you will generally want to increase it about 25%.

In the same way, 20% of 20% is 4%. So if you're working at 20%, you will want to increase the effect about 4%. And if you want a little more, then 20% of 24% is approximately 5%, and so on. The keyboard command for changing the opacity of a brush is: 100% opacity is 0, 50% is 5, 20% is 2, and 10 is 1. (Hence the name 0521 rule).

Being in Two Places at Once

What follows is a way to have both the image on which you are working and the layer mask of that image visible at full size on the screen at the same time:

Go to the Window Menu > Arrange > and select the New Window for (image name) from the bottom of the menu. This opens a new window of the same image that is "Live." After each stroke, that window will be updated so you can see the effect of each change you make.

Put the two images side by side (or if you use dual monitors, put one image on each monitor), and Alt/Option-click on the layer mask of whichever of the images has the layer mask you want to show. Now, depending on whether you want to work on the image or the layer mask, make that image active, and you will be able to see what happens as you do your brush work (**Figure 1.13**).

Error-Free Layer Masks

Now that you have a layer mask, wouldn't be nice to have one that has no missed areas or unwanted overlaps? Here's how.

The important thing to remember, as I discussed in the 80/20 Rule, is that when you are working on a layer mask, you are working in grayscale. This means that

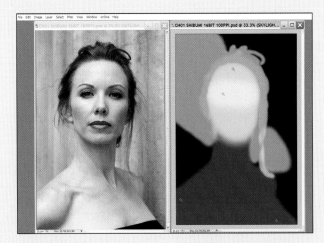

when you change the opacity of white or black (depending on whether you are revealing or concealing), you are changing the density of the color with which you are working. That change in density manifests itself as shades of gray on the layer mask.

As I discussed in the 0521 Rule, there is an interrelationship between 100, 50, 20 and 10% when you are working with opacity on a layer mask. The problem is that when you brush over something, you might miss an area. If you brush the way most people do, brushing is cumulative. So it's almost impossible to match up the areas you missed with the areas that you didn't. Rather than try the conventional approach to brushing, treat the layer mask as a color, the color gray.

Approach 1: Make the layer mask visible at full screen (See the Being in Two Places at Once section of this sidebar.) and make the layer mask active. Select the brush tool and set the brush opacity at 100%. Alt/Option-click on the area that you want to sample (the Alt/Option key brings up the sample tool eyedropper when you are in the brush tool), and brush over the area you missed or in which you have an unwanted overlap. (Remember, you are painting with gray.)

Approach 2: Set the brush opacity to 100%. Alt/Option-click on the area that you want to sample. Select the Polygonal lasso tool. (The keyboard command is the letter L. If you want to scroll through any tool, hold down the Shift key and click on the tool's letter until the desired tool appears.) Mouse click around the area and, when you have the desired area selected, Alt+Backspace or Option+Delete to fill with the foreground color.

Approach 3: (The Peter Bauer Method)

1. In order to make the layer (rather than the mask) active, click on the layer thumbnail to the left in the Layers palette.
2. Layer > Layer Style > Stroke. (The default color is red, so stick with red as the color unless the image has a lot of red.) Increase the stroke width to 10 or 15 pixels.
3. Click OK in the Layer Style dialog box.
4. Click on the layer mask thumbnail to the right in the Layers palette.
5. Where you see blobs of red in the image, there are stray black or white areas, so (with the layer mask active) simply paint over the red spots with the appropriate color and watch them go away.
6. After cleaning up the mask, delete (or hide until next time) the Stroke layer style.

Step 5: Creating Selective Depth of Field

When I talked about creating the image map for depth of field, one of the issues I addressed was that I wanted the back wall to appear lit as if it was positioned well behind the subject. What I actually photographed was a subject standing up against the wall. If I could have cross-lit the background, I would have positioned the subject about 5 feet from the wall. To create a believable probability, I had to add the illusion of optical depth. You will do that by creating a layer of blur between two layers of sharpness.

1. Turn off the Skylight layer by clicking on the eyeball (located next to layer). Duplicate the MASTER 1 layer and rename the duplicate layer D OF F BLUR (for Depth of Field Blur).

2. Go to Filter > Blur > Gaussian Blur and choose a radius of 12 pixels. Click OK.

NOTE: The amount of Gaussian blur you apply to an image is in direct relationship to the size of the image. The bigger the file, the greater the amount of blur you need to apply to get the same effect.

3. With the D OF F BLUR layer still active, turn on the D OF F IM layer.

4. Create a black-filled layer mask on the D OF F BLUR layer.

5. Turn on the D OF F image map.

6. Select a soft brush 500 pixels wide, which is the distance between the two catchlights in the subject's eyes.

NOTE: Use the edge of the brush to paint from the top of the head (marked 50% on the image map) all the way around the hair, with the brush's edge following the left edge of the outer hairline and down the shoulder. Make sure to color within the lines on the image map.

7. When you have painted in the left side of the image, start again from the top of the image and go over that area again, but this time start parallel to the left cheek (seen from your point of view). Now set the brush opacity at 20% and make the brush two sizes smaller. Repeat the process on the right side of the background, moving from the top of the head to the lower right corner. Set the brush opacity at 10% and repeat the same process in the torso area under the neck.

8. Save the file (**Figures 1.14a**, **1.14b**, and **1.14c**).

FIGURE 1.14A *The D of F image map.*

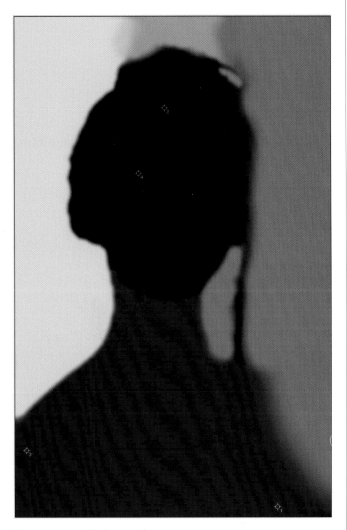

FIGURE 1.14B *The layer mask.*

FIGURE 1.14C *The combined layers that cause the illusion of depth of field.*

Light Changes Ahead

Up to this point, the modifications to the image have been profound, but subtle. From here on, they will be more dramatic. By removing such issues as color cast and the lack of depth of field, which would otherwise be problems throughout the image editing process, you have created an image with which you can more easily work. In other words, you've been working from global to granular.

Now it's time to start building the "lighting" of this image. Remember, you are in service of reality, and the changes you make to an image must be transparent to the viewer. This means paying attention to the way light manifests itself in the real world. Light has a direction, and so do any shadows it casts. Fail to respect that physical law, and the result will look like those paintings you see in mall "art" stores—cutesy pictures of snow-covered cottages with light shining from 17 different places at once.

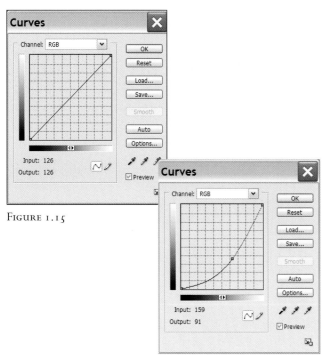

FIGURE 1.15

FIGURE 1.16 *Adjusting the curve.*

Step 6: Creating Light-to-Dark Using Curves Adjustment Layers

Your work on this image is cumulative; one modification builds on the last. This step in the lighting process addresses the light-to-dark aspect of how the eye "sees" an image.

As a practical matter, it makes sense to tackle the depth of field problem before doing light-to-dark. It's a lot easier to see the effect of depth of field while the image is light.

1. Create a Curves adjustment layer above the SKYLIGHT layer (**Figure 1.15**).

2. Click the center point of the line that runs across the curves dialog and drag the point down in a diagonal. Don't flatten or "clip" the bottom part of the curve, and click OK (**Figure 1.16**).

NOTE: To get the small gridlines, which give you a finer degree of control, Alt-/Option-click on the grid.

3. Name the layer L2D (Light to Dark).

The image's color has now changed, because when you darken a color, it increases in saturation (**Figure 1.17**). This isn't something you necessarily want. You just spent a lot of time addressing the file's color issues, and now you have a new one on your hands. To correct this, I recommend you switch the blending mode from Normal to Luminosity. The Luminosity blending mode deals only with the light-to-dark aspect, or luminance of the image, and leaves the colors alone.

4. Go to the top of the Layers palette and choose Luminosity from the Blending Mode menu. You should notice that the image is now less saturated (**Figure 1.18**).

NOTE: Sometimes you may want to make an image more saturated. If you like the way it looks, you can leave the blending mode in Normal. You're the only person you should ever have to please.

5. Turn on the L2D image map and make the L2D Curves adjustment layer active. Select a soft 500-pixel brush at 100% opacity. You are going to paint in the area of the face you want to be the lightest; (V-Semicolon) or the one at 100%. Then repeat the process with the hair, torso, and background,

increasing and decreasing the brush sizes and opacity as you did in the previous steps (**Figures 1.19**, **1.20**, and **1.21**).

6. If you haven't done so already, turn off the L2D IL image map. Make the L2D Curves adjustment layer active, and do "The Move." Name the resulting layer MASTER 2, and save the file.

FIGURE 1.19 *The light-to-dark image map.*

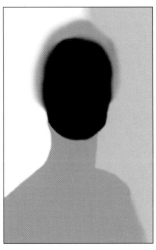

FIGURE 1.20 *The L 2 D LUM adjustment layer mask.*

FIGURE 1.17 *The image in Normal blending mode.*

FIGURE 1.18 *In Luminosity mode, colors are less saturated.*

FIGURE 1.21 *The result of selectively changing the light-to-dark ratio.*

Step 7: Lighting the Image with Render > Lighting Effects

Every time you do something in Photoshop, you are "dumping" or "clipping" data and creating artifacts. If you shoot in the RAW file format, the original file is the least artifacted and in the cleanest data state it ever will be.

Because artifacts are cumulative, eventually enough data will be affected that those artifacts will become visible. So the key is to build into your workflow an approach that minimizes artifacts and affords you an exit strategy. One way to insure the former, minimizing artifacts, is to do as much work as possible in 16-bit. In the case of this image, we did everything we could before we ran into something that couldn't be done at 16-bit. So to move forward requires us to convert the file to 8-bit. The payoff? Whatever artifacts we have created will be lost or minimized in the conversion process.

Go to Image > Mode > 8 bits/Channel, and click it. "Save As" and rename the file (Ctrl-Shift-S/Cmd-Shift-S). Keep the same file name but add "8 bit" after the name and before the file type (.TIF, .psd, etc.). For example, SHIBUMI 16 BIT.PSD would become SHIBUMI 8 BIT.PSD. That way, you always leave an exit strategy in place, which you have been building into the workflow of this file from the very beginning.

Using Render > Lighting Effects

You are now going to work with the Render > Lighting Effects filter to make the image look as if you had used the appropriate lighting when the image was shot. First, you will light the background, and then the subject, using key light, and then fill light. Once the "lights" are placed, you'll adjust the intensity.

Because this is a filter that you will use in almost every chapter of this book, let's take a look at how it's set up before you begin.

NOTE: To view this filter go to Filter > Render > Lighting Effects (**Figure 1.22a**).

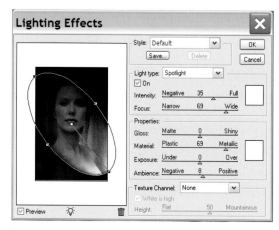

FIGURE 1.22A *The Render > Lighting Effects filter dialog box.*

On the right side of the of the dialog box, from top to bottom, the first thing you see is the Style pull-down menu. This menu contains a series of 16 presets—ranging from the default, which is "Spotlight," to multiple lights like "Five Down" or colored lighting effects like "RGB."

NOTE: The styles, such as "Soft Spotlight" and "Soft Omni" are presets that use specific settings. Interestingly, re-creating those settings to get the same effect requires a very deft touch. I've found it's better to start with a preset and then adjust the settings or add more lights as each image requires.

You can also save the lighting set up you create by using the Save button. This will save what you've done as a preset. Doing this is a good idea, because, as you will experience when working with an image, the graphic user interface of this plug-in is difficult because the preview window is exceptionally small. So using this filter in its current form requires some degree of trial and error. Saving the lighting setup that you are working on allows you to come back and readjust things if you don't get it exactly as you'd like it the first time. For this lesson, I have included saving the lighting setups as presets. By doing this, you will have both an exit strategy and a way to practice at practicing. You just

need to remember to clear out the presets you've created from time to time.

You can check the intensity of a single light by making that light the active one and then clicking off the "On" box located just under the Light type pull-down menu.

Next is the "Light type" menu. This works in tandem with, but is different from, the Style pull-down menu. In this menu, you can choose three different types of "light": Spotlight, Omni, and Directional.

NOTE: The best way to conceptualize these three types of light is this:

Directional: is a distant light with parallel rays. (The light does not diffuse over distance.)

Omni: is omnidirectional light, the type of light you see when there is a bare bulb hanging over a poker table.

Spotlight: throws an elliptical beam whose direction, focus, intensity, and size you can control.

In general, I have found that using Omni or Spotlight creates studio lighting effects that most closely replicate a believable probability. Usually, you either want a downward directed light source (Omni) or you want an angled beam (Spotlight). However, when I'm trying replicate the look and feel of natural sunlight, Directional gives a result that looks like sun shining through a window.

In addition to the pull-down menu, this dialog box has two sliders. The first is Intensity, and it moves from Negative to Full. This increases and decreases the specific brightness of the light source that you are trying to adjust. The second is Focus (used only with the Spotlight option), and it determines how much of the elliptical area is filled with light. When the Spotlight area is round, 50% is half the diameter; 100% fills the circle. When the Spotlight area is elliptical, the center is halfway along the line from the center to the light source, and the value determines how much of that area is filled. This slider defines the width of the specific "light" that you are adjusting.

Moving downward, the next area of the Render Lighting Effects Filter dialog box is the Properties dialog box. This box has four sliders. The first one, Gloss, ranges from Matte to Shiny, and the second one, Material, ranges from Plastic to Metallic. The Gloss slider determines the reflectivity of the "surface" on which you're applying the filter. The Material slider determines what will be reflected, the light or the surface. Plastic uses the light's color in the reflection, while metallic uses the object's color in the reflection. The last two sliders, Exposure and Ambience, are properties of the "surface" upon which your created light is falling. Exposure addresses the general brightness of the image to which you are applying the Lighting Effects filter. Ambience determines how much lighting exists in the scene other than your added light. Another way to think about Ambience is it governs the light outside of the ellipse or circle.

NOTE: For both the Light type and the Exposure menus, there is a white box located to the right of the sliders. If you double-click on a swatch, you'll open the Color Picker. This allows you to select colors for the light that you're adding (Light type), as well as for the ambient light (Properties).

To change the position of a light, click on the center dot of the light and drag it to the position that you want. You change the size of a light by clicking on one of its four anchor points, or dots, and dragging them to increase or decrease the size or change the shape of the light. (You can also rotate the position of the light by clicking on one of these points and rotating the light in the direction of choice.)

To create a new light, click on the light bulb, located in the middle beneath the image preview, and drag it to the area you want. Then, in the Light type pull-down menu, select either Spotlight, Omni, or Directional.

To make a light active, click on the center point of the light on which you want to work.

To remove a light, make the light you want to remove active and drag it to the Trash Can icon, located next to the Create a New Light icon (the lightbulb).

Creating the Background Light

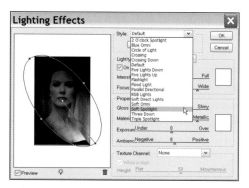

FIGURE 1.22B

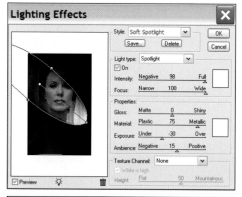

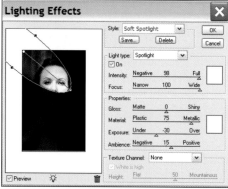

1. Duplicate the layer MASTER 2 and rename it BG LIGHTING. Make the LIGHTING IM image map active.

2. Go to Filter > Render > Lighting Effects. On the Style menu, select Soft Spotlight (**Figure 1.22b**).

3. Click on the center of the Spotlight, and move the light to the upper-left corner of the preview area (**Figures 1.23a** and **1.23b**).

4. Click the lower anchor point of the spotlight and drag it to the edge of the upper left part of the gray area of the image preview box (**Figure 1.24a**).

5. Next, click on the middle anchor point and rotate the light until the line that connects the two crosses through the middle of the model's nose. Now, under Properties, move the Gloss Slider to Matte and the Material Slider to Metalllic (**Figures 1.24b** and **1.24c**).

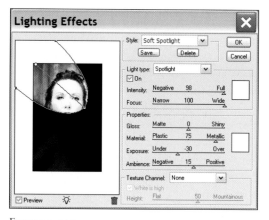

FIGURE 1.24A

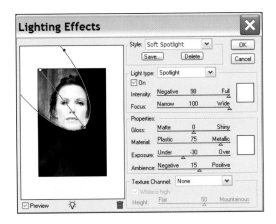

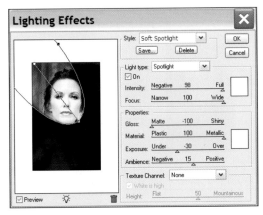

FIGURES 1.24B AND 1.24C

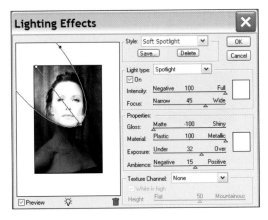

FIGURE 1.24D

NOTE: Notice that the light has become more diffuse and less intense. Also, the face is so completely lit that it is almost blown out. That's okay. Our concern at the moment is the way the light looks on the wall behind the subject. (You will address the issue of lighting the subject on a different layer.) Because you began this process knowing what you wanted at its end, you can work with small pieces of what will go to create the final image. Being able to previsualize, seeing the end first, means that all of your choices are informed ones. Simply put, never losing sight of the end (the print), the more you know about the middle, the more informed your choices can be at the beginning.

6. Now, in the same Properties menu, change the Exposure slider to 32 and the Ambience slider to 15. Next, move up to the Light type and set the focus to 45. What you have just created is the background light of this image (**Figure 1.24d**).

7. Click the lightbulb under the image. Drag and drop the light parallel to the middle of the left ear and right on the edge of the image (**Figure 1.25a**).

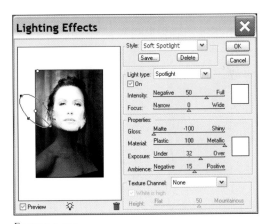

FIGURE 1.25A

8. Click the upper anchor point, and drag it until it is a circle and the anchor point is right on her hairline (**Figure 1.25b**). Set the Intensity to 17 and the Focus to 39 (**Figure 1.25c**).

9. Click the lightbulb under the image again, then drag and drop a light just to the right of the neck and just below her chin (**Figure 1.26a**). Click on the upper anchor point, drag it until it is parallel to the bottom of the nose. Set the Intensity to 21 and the Focus to –29 (**Figure 1.26b**).

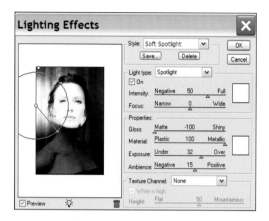

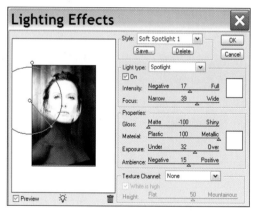

FIGURES 1.25B AND 1.25C

NOTE: At this point, I saved this lighting set up as a preset and named it "Soft Spot 1." Notice that there is a definable line between the first and second lights that you created. Although their placement and intensity is pleasing, you need to blend them better. By saving this grouping as a preset, if you make choices that you don't like as you go on, you can always go back to the last step that you did like. Since I determined the light settings that I've chosen for this lesson by trial and error, by saving each of them as presets, I built an exit strategy into my workflow and allowed myself the chance to practice at practicing.

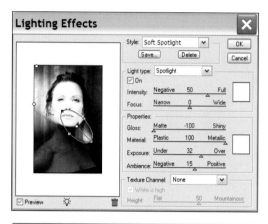

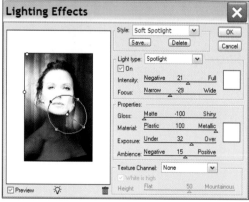

FIGURES 1.26A AND 1.26B

Figure 1.26c

Adjusting the Intensity of the Background Lights

You now need to balance the lights. With some frequency, you will find that after you place lights, they may not blend as smoothly as you would like. To fix this, you will go back to each individual light and fine-tune it.

10. Click on the center point of the first light you dropped down on the image, making it the active light. Lower the intensity to 71. Now, make the second light you laid down active. Set the Intensity to 25, the Focus to 35, the Exposure to 21, and the Ambience to 15. Save this setting as a preset and name it Soft Spot 2, then click OK. What you should have is something that looks like this (**Figure 1.26c**).

NOTE: Unless you quit out of Photoshop, Photoshop will preserve the lighting choices you have made. So if you click OK and find the result that you have does not look as "okay" as it did in the preview, you can Cmd-/Ctrl-Z to undo the change and go back and readjust the lights. If you don't like that adjustment, you can always start over because you have saved the settings before you made any changes.

Brushing in the Background Lights

1. Create a Layer mask on the layer BG LIGHTING and fill the layer mask with black.

NOTE: For all of the layer mask work that you will be doing in this book, it's easier to have both the image and the layer mask visible and active at the same time. To see how to do this, refer to the "Unmasking Layer Masks" sidebar earlier in this chapter.

2. Making the foreground color white (following the lighting image map), brush the torso and the background light to the right of Challen's neck at an opacity of 25%.

FIGURE 1.27 *After the background lights have been brushed in.*

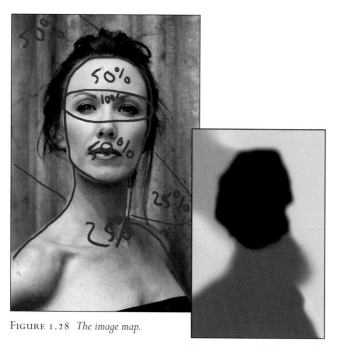

FIGURE 1.28 *The image map.*

FIGURE 1.29 *The layer mask.*

3. Brush in the shaft of light behind Challen's head at an opacity of 50%, and the areas on either side of that light shaft as well as the rest of the background, at 75%. What you should have is an image and its accompanying layer mask that look like this (**Figures 1.27**, **1.28**, and **1.29**).

Creating the Key/Fill Light

Now it's time to light Challen's face. Just as you did with the background lighting, you are going to build up the key and fill lights, working from global to granular. First you will place the lights, then you will adjust their intensity and brightness.

NOTE: The purpose of the key light is to light the area of the eyes, making this area the lightest part of the image. Since the unconscious eye's tendency is to go first to light areas, the viewer's eye will start at the face as you had planned it should.

Creating the Key Light

1. Duplicate the MASTER 2 layer, name the copy KEY/FILL LIGHT, and move it above the BG LIGHTING layer.

2. Go to Filter > Render > Lighting Effects. In the Style menu, select Soft Omni. Click the center point of this light and move it so that the center point is between the top of the left eyelid and the eyebrow. Now, click on the outer left anchor point and reduce the circle until its outer edge is on the outer part of the subject's hair (**Figure 1.30a**).

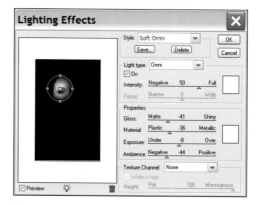

FIGURE 1.30A

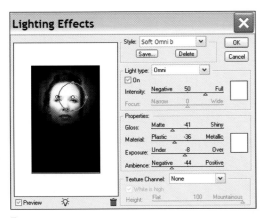

Figure 1.30b

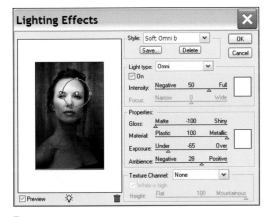

Figure 1.30c

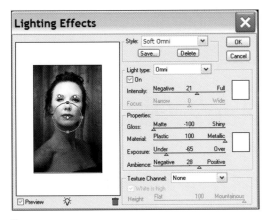

Figure 1.31

NOTE: The reason for using Soft Omni instead of Soft Spotlight, as you did in creating the background light, is that you want a softer, more diffused light that is not directional. Also, you want the light to appear as if it is in front of and slightly above the subject.

3. Click the lightbulb located directly underneath the image and, in the Light type menu, select Omni. Drag it to just above the model's right eye and just below her eyebrow. Click on the right anchor point and make this light the same size as the first one (**Figure 1.30b**).

4. In the Lighting Effects dialog, set the gloss to –100 (Matte), and Material to 100 (Metallic). Now, decrease the exposure to –65 and the ambience to 28 (**Figure 1.30c**).

NOTE: There are two reasons for making these choices.

First, you want the lights to be of equal intensity, so they both have to be the same size. It's easier to place them first than to choose their types first.

Second, you want the light to appear diffused, so you set the property of that type of light to soft (Matte). The light should appear as if it were focused, so there will be a hardness to its edges, which is why you chose 100 (Metallic) for material.

Adding the Fill Light

Now that you have placed and coarsely adjusted the key light, it's time to place the fill lights. You will use fill lights to add light to those areas of the face in which you want shadows that contain visual detail.

5. Click the lightbulb located directly underneath the image and drag it so that its center point is directly on the subject's lower lip. Under Light Type, select Omni. Click on the lower anchor point and reduce the size of the light until the bottom of the circle touches the bottom of the subject's chin. Diminish the intensity to 21 (**Figure 1.31**).

Adjusting the Key and Fill Lights

It's time to dial in the key and fill lights. The first issues are that the forehead is very hot and the key light is more intense on the left than the right.

First, reduce the overall exposure to –75 and the Ambience to 39. Make the right eye light active and increase the intensity to 89. Save this lighting group as a preset and name it Soft Omni 1. Click OK (**Figures 1.32a** and **1.32b**).

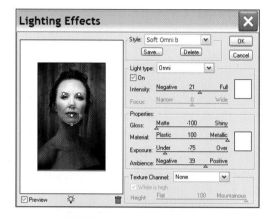

FIGURES 1.32A AND 1.32B *The key and fill light effect.*

Brushing in the Key and Fill Lights

1. Create a Layer mask on the layer BG LIGHTING and fill the layer mask with black.

2. You will now build relationships of intensity among areas of the image in much the same way that you did when you corrected for color cast earlier (**Figures 1.33** and **1.34a**).

3. Create a layer mask and fill it with black.

4. Select a 300-pixel brush (the distance from the eyebrow to the bottom of the eye socket) at an opacity of 20%. Brush the eyes, then the rest of the face. Set the brush opacity at 50% and brush the forehead, above the area that we marked as 100%, across the eyes, and the lower area, including the torso. Increase the brush size to 500 pixels. Starting at the top of the image in the middle, brush the entire right side, going clockwise until just under the background light on the left.

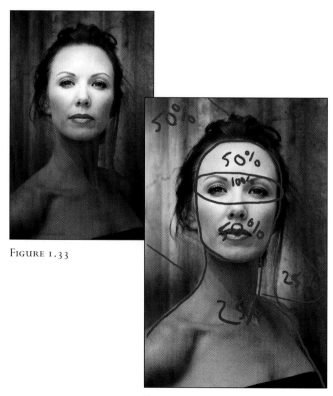

FIGURE 1.33

FIGURE 1.34A

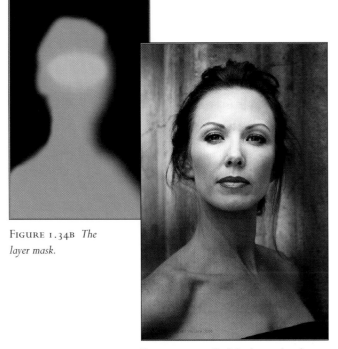

FIGURE 1.34B *The layer mask.*

FIGURE 1.34C *Both background and key/fill light layers.*

FIGURE 1.35 *The blown-out areas of the face from the Render > Lighting Effects filter.*

5. As noted before, when you darken color you change saturation. You don't want that here, so change the blending modes on both the BG LIGHTING 1 and the KEY LIGHT layers from Normal to Luminosity (**Figures 1.34b** and **1.34c**).

6. Turn off the image map layer, make the KEY LIGHT layer active, and merge these layers together by doing "The Move." Name the new layer MASTER 3 and save the document.

Step 8: Bending, Not Breaking Pixels: Addressing the Sins of Our Artifacts

Whenever you do anything in Photoshop, you are altering the data. When the data is altered, some of it is clipped or dropped and forever lost. That is how artifacts are created. As I have already discussed, artifacting is cumulative, and if you accumulate enough artifacts, you will see them in your image. In other words, you have performed so many manipulations that you have bent the pixels to the point of breaking them.

The goal of anything you do in Photoshop is to make it look like you didn't do anything at all. So if someone asks, "Did you *do* something in Photoshop?" you want it to be a question rather than an accusation. You want to use Photoshop as an emery board and not a jackhammer. However, there are times when no amount of care can prevent artifact formation. This step is about how to address blown-out areas (a type of artifacting) that sometimes results from using the Render > Lighting Effects filter. The areas in question are the ridge of the nose and area of the left cheek just below the eye (**Figure 1.35**).

FIGURE 1.36

FIGURE 1.37

Correcting the Blown-Out Area of the Cheek

1. Make the MASTER 3 layer active.

2. Select the Move tool and turn on Rulers (Ctrl-R/Cmd-R) if they are off. Go to the left side of the screen and drag a guide line to the center of the image. Place guides to the right and left of the highest point of the check bones. From the top ruler, place guides at the top of the highest points of the lips and the middle of her pupils (**Figure 1.36**).

3. Select the Marquee tool. Click the upper part of the right box that you created with the guides and drag it to the lower outside corner (**Figure 1.37**).

4. Copy this selection to its own layer (Ctrl-J/Cmd-J). Go to Edit > Transform > Flip Horizontal (**Figure 1.38**). Using the Move tool, slide the flipped selection to the left side of the face, lining up its inside edge to the center guide.

NOTE: The keyboard command for doing Free Transform is Ctrl-T/Cmd-T, which brings up the Free Transform box. Right-click on the selection. This brings up the Free Transform menu. Select Flip Horizontal. If you use the keyboard shortcut, you can also do the next step at the same time.

FIGURE 1.38 *The flipped selection is about to be moved.*

5. Choose Edit > Free Transform (Ctrl-T/Cmd-T). While holding the Control/Command key down, click the center-left handle and drag the selection until the bottom part of the cheek of our selection lines up with the cheek of the MASTER 4 layer. Press Enter/Return to apply the transform (**Figure 1.39**).

6. Create a layer mask filled with black, and zoom into the area of the left cheek. Select the Brush tool with a size of 90 pixels (the diameter of the iris) at an opacity of 75% and brush the area of the cheek that looks slightly "hot" or blown out. Name this layer CHEEK (**Figures 1.40**, **1.41**, and **1.42**).

NOTE: You could also fix the cheek with the Patch tool, but in my experience, the Patch tool doesn't always work well, especially on a face. Real pixels usually look better than "trans-morphed" pixels.

7. Bring the image to full screen and name the new layer CHEEK.

FIGURE 1.40 *Before.*

FIGURE 1.41 *After.*

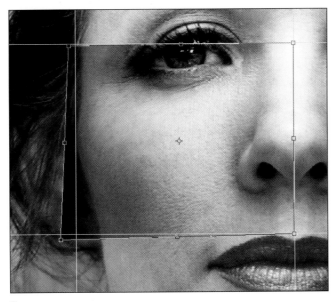

FIGURE 1.39

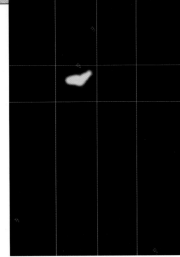

FIGURE 1.42 *The layer mask.*

FIGURE 1.43 *Before.*

FIGURE 1.44 *After.*

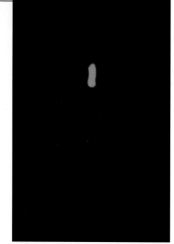

FIGURE 1.45 *The layer mask.*

Correcting the Blown-Out Area of the Cheek

8. Duplicate the MASTER 2 layer and move it so that it is above the CHEEK layer. Make sure it's the active layer and create a layer mask. Fill that layer mask with black and, using the same 90-pixel brush, paint in the area of the nose with white at an opacity of 75%. Name this layer NOSE (**Figures 1.43, 1.44**, and **1.45**).

Do "The Move," name the new layer MASTER 4, and save the file.

Step 9: Creating a Realistic Shadow

The most common way to make a shadow or drop shadow is to make a new layer, create a selection, feather that selection, fill that selection with black, zap it with Gaussian blur, and then lower the opacity. This is fine when you are working with fonts and such, but the result often doesn't look real when you are working with things that are three-dimensional. One of the major considerations in putting a shadow into your composition is the direction from which the light is striking your subject. This will influence the size and position of the shadow that you would expect to see. If you don't take this into account, you run the risk of creating images where the light may appear to be coming from several different directions at once. This results in images that are unrealistic. In this step, you will create a realistic-looking shadow.

NOTE: See also "Add a Butterfly Shadow," in Chapter 4.

1. Zoom in on the model's nose and mouth (**Figure 1.46**).

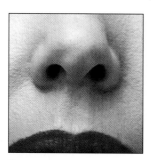

FIGURE 1.46

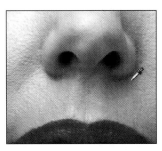

FIGURES 1.47 AND 1.48 *Sampling the shadow color and the color sampler.*

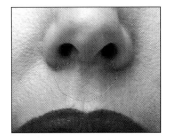

FIGURES 1.49 AND 1.50

FIGURE 1.51 *The shadow.*

FIGURE 1.52 *The layer mask.*

2. With the Eyedropper tool, sample the color of the shadow just below the right side of the nose, so that the foreground color now reflects the color of the shadow (**Figures 1.47** and **1.48**).

3. Create a new layer and name it SHADOW.

4. With the Polygonal Lasso tool, select a lock point that starts at the edge of the shadow below the nose (**Figure 1.49**). Mouse-click a selection, go to Select > Feather, select a 10-pixel radius, and click OK. Fill the selection with the foreground color (Alt-Backspace/Option-Delete), deselect the selection (click on the layer), then open the Gaussian Blur filter and choose a radius of 15 pixels (**Figure 1.50**).

NOTE: The radius of the feather should be in direct relationship to the size of the area being feathered, as well as the size and resolution of the file. The bigger the file or the area selected, the bigger the radius.

5. Go to the Layers palette and lower the opacity of this layer until it matches the intensity of the shadow from which you sampled the color. In this case, that's 68%.

6. Add a layer mask filled with white in order to paint with black (because you want to reveal 80% and conceal 20%), and touch up the shadow. Select a reasonably small brush, about 60 pixels. Using the edge of the brush at 50% opacity, smooth the top and the right side of the shadow (**Figures 1.51** and **1.52**).

FIGURE 1.53 *The final shadow.*

7. Bring the image to full-screen mode for the final adjustment to the shadow's opacity. For this image, that means taking it from 68% to 45% (**Figure 1.53**).

8. Do "The Move," name the new layer MASTER 4, and save the file (**Figure 1.54**).

FIGURE 1.54 *The final image.*

The Transformation
Is Complete

This lesson is about learning how to be in Shibumi whenever and wherever you create, and about developing a dynamic, proactive way of thinking about workflow.

As I discussed at the beginning of this chapter, practice doesn't make perfect, perfect practice makes perfect. What you need to do is practice at practicing. So before you move on to the next chapter, I suggest you begin with the original image and repeat the entire process described in this lesson. Then try to do it without referring to the lesson. Lastly, try it without using image maps, and see how fast and accurate you can get. What I have found on my journey as an artist is that to truly gain mastery of anything, simple repetition was not the answer. Rather, you need to engage in exercising variations of what you are repeating. In that way, your technique evolves and grows. In other words, you need to engage in the exercise of repetition until you are in Shibumi, and with Shibumi comes mastery and the achievement of perfect practice.

FIGURE 2.1 *Before.*

FIGURE 2.2 Hearing the Whisper of the Green Fairy.

Chapter 2

Image Harvesting

Precision does not mean accuracy. Precision is just the number of decimal points back.
Accuracy is how well precision reflects reality.

—Lane H. Decker

In this chapter, we will explore the concept of *image harvesting*. This is the practice of shooting multiple images of the same subject while changing the exposure, shutter speed, and focus point. This guarantees that your source files will contain the optimum aesthetic aspects of exposure, depth of field, and focus, so that you can later combine them to create a single, final image.

Recreating What the Eye Saw

The human eye is a multipurpose organic optical system. As an organic optical system, it can discern detail in light as dim as moonlight and as bright as noon's direct sunlight at the equator. It also acts as a motion sensor, sees events as they happen, and sees everything in focus while adjusting for changes in the intensity of light. Also, it does all of this in real time.

A digital still camera, on the other hand, is not a multipurpose, organic optical system with all the capabilities of the human eye. It is simply an image-capturing device that records a very small part of what we see. It records only fractions of seconds, while the vast majority of what we see is felt and witnessed in motion. The human eye is capable of adjusting for changes in light and has the ability to determine detail in both extremely low- and high-light situations. Cameras, on the other hand, always seek to expose for 18% gray. This means that if you were to take a picture of a white wall and then a black wall, when viewed neither image would be black or white; they both would be 18% gray. Additionally, no matter how sensitive the light meter in the camera, it cannot determine what area of the image is the most important. There is no camera that comes with an automatic subject finder. Only the photographer can determine what is important in the image.

So the question becomes, "How do I replicate what I saw with a device that doesn't record the image the way I felt and experienced it when I saw and shot it?" The answer is fairly straightforward. Rather than shoot one image and hope for the best, consider harvesting many images and combining them into one. This is the best way I know to create an image that looks like what the eye saw—not just what the camera captured.

Practicing "Preemptive Photoshop"

The image that will be the outcome of this lesson, *Hearing the Whisper of the Green Fairy* (**Figure 2.2**), was "harvested" rather than simply shot with one image. I captured 87 images, and out of those, four were chosen. There were so many captures because some were shot at different exposures, some at different focus points, and some were a combination of both. What I was practicing when I was capturing these images was "preemptive Photoshop"—making informed decisions so that I got it "right" in the camera at the time of capture. Having done this, I would later use Photoshop as an emery board rather than a jackhammer. Consider approaching Photoshop as a noun and not a verb. Don't operate on the belief that you can always "fix it" in Photoshop. At best, you can only hope to save a photograph that was impetuously shot. Photoshop is only a means to the end. Your goal should always be to get it right in the camera. But when the camera cannot give you your vision, adapt to the needs of the situation and get as much right in camera as you can. Because the camera's capabilities limit you, you must give yourself as many choices as you can when you are taking the picture, so that when it comes time to work on the image at the computer you are not limited by captures you lack. I have also found that real pixels are infinitely better than artificially generated ones. The image that I chose as the main, or "base," image for this lesson was one in which I liked the relationship between its main point of focus—the leaf in the upper part of the picture—and the overall image. From the three other captures, I took those parts that I felt resolved those areas in the "base" image that were issues for me. The issue areas were the leaf in the foreground, the cluster of other leaves in the mid-ground, and the absence of interesting detail in the background. After making the composite, I enhanced it as if it were a single image.

Before you dive into all that follows, think about whether you are creating a believable improbability or a believable probability. Ponder this as you work your way through this lesson.

NOTE: If you have not already done so, go to www.Niksoftware.com/ozlessons and download the Skylight and Contrast filters. You might want to download the Sharpener Pro demo as well.

Photoshop Setup and Workflow

As with any image, the first steps are to analyze the image, determine which problems need to be addressed, and decide on the appropriate workflow. As discussed earlier, workflow is a dynamic thing and is specific to each image. In image harvesting, you first choose the images you will use, then:

- Fix any problems with the base image.
- Combine the desired elements taken from the other images.
- Do color correction and aesthetic image manipulation.

It's wise to solve the biggest problems first. Here, for example, the biggest issue isn't correcting the color cast of all four images; it's getting one image from the four. It's easier to color correct one final image than to color correct each image separately.

Try to develop a workflow that minimizes artifacting. Every time you do something in Photoshop, you are clipping or dumping some amount of data. This causes artifacts. While some of these are visually appealing, some are not. And all artifacting is cumulative. One way to minimize this is to work in 16-bit. This image's workflow is approached with that in mind.

Here are the four harvested images that make up the palette for this lesson:

- Image 1: This is the base image, which contains the central focus point of the final image, the large leaf at the top (the primary focus area) (**Figure 2.3a**).
- Image 2: A nearly identical photo with the focus on a cluster of leaves beneath the large leaf at the top (the secondary focus area) (**Figure 2.3b**).
- Image 3: A slightly different image, where a single leaf below the cluster is in focus (the tertiary focus area) (**Figure 2.3c**).
- Image 4: An image taken from a different angle that contains three leaves in focus and a nice pattern for the background (**Figure 2.3d**).

This is the image map of what you will be doing (**Figure 2.3e**).

FIGURE 2.3A *Image 1: the base image.*

FIGURE 2.3B *Image 2: focus on the leaf cluster.*

FIGURE 2.3C *Image 3: focus on a single leaf.*

FIGURE 2.3D *Image 4: interesting background.*

FIGURE 2.3E *The harvesting image map.*

Creating the Composite Image

Step 1: Combining the Four Images into One

All of the image manipulation decisions you will make, including those concerning creating one image out of four, will be made based on the way the eye works when it "sees." As was discussed in Chapter 1, the eye goes to patterns that it recognizes first, areas of light to dark, high contrast to low contrast, high sharpness to low sharpness, in focus to blur (which is different from high sharpness to low sharpness), and high saturation of color to low saturation of color. When working on an image, correct from global to granular. Always solve the biggest problems first and work down to the smallest.

1. Go to the folder on the DVD Ch02, using BANFF0273.tif as the base file, double-click the background layer, and rename it BASE IMAGE. One at a time, shift-click and drag the image icon in the Layers palette from the three harvested images to the base image.

By using the shift-click method, the copied image will pin register with the base image. In other words, Photoshop will place the copied image exactly on top of the base image. Here is the layer order, from the bottom up:

BASE IMAGE:	This was BANFF0274.tif.
MID LEAVES:	This was BANFF0273.tif.
FG LEAF:	This was BANFF0277.tif.
BG PARTS:	This was BANFF0269.tif.

2. Close the BANFF0273.tif, BANFF0277.tif, and BANFF0269.tif files. They are no longer needed.

3. Save the file (Shift-Ctrl-S/Shift-Cmd-S) as a Photoshop or .psd file (not as a layered Tiff) and name it GREEN FAIRY 16BIT.

NOTE: Photoshop should be set to Snap To Guides (on the View > Snap To menu), and the viewing mode to Full Screen with Menu Bar. Keyboard shortcut F displays the image on top of a neutral gray background.

Step 2: Removing Unwanted Elements from the Base Image

In the base image, the viewer's eye is drawn away from the main leaf by a distracting branch. This is the biggest problem, because it will show up in everything that you do until you remove it. You will do this by using the Patch tool (**Figure 2.4a**).

FIGURE 2.4A *The distracting branch.*

FIGURE 2.4B *The branch is removed.*

FIGURE 2.5A *The area of sharp focus in Image 1.*

FIGURE 2.5B *The area of sharp focus in Image 2.*

1. Make a copy of the BASE IMAGE layer (Ctrl-J/Cmd-J) and name it PATCH.

2. Select the Patch tool (J) and choose Source in the Options bar.

NOTE: When selecting a tool, hold down the Shift key while pressing its shortcut key to cycle through the tools having that same shortcut key.

3. Make sure the Transparent box is not checked. Zoom in on the area to be affected. Using the Patch tool, select the unwanted branch. Don't select any of the leaf that overlaps the branch; the Patch tool could create unwanted artifacts in this area. The rest of the branch will be fixed later with the Healing Brush or Clone Stamp tool.

4. Drag the selection (the source) to an acceptable alternative area—in this case, the area just below the branch.

5. Use the Clone Stamp tool (S) to remove the remainder of the branch next to the leaf. Choose a soft 50-pixel brush and clone out the branch around the leaf until the unwanted areas are removed. Alt/Option-click multiple source points to avoid creating a repeating pattern.

6. Repeat the process with both the Patch and the Clone Stamp tools to remove the other unwanted remaining bits of the branch (**Figure 2.04b**).

Step 3: Correcting the Shallow Depth of Field

I chose the base image because I liked the way the leaf in the upper part of the composition (the central focal point) related to the overall image. But the image was shot at f/5.6, so its depth of field is fairly shallow, and the mid and foreground are out of focus. You will correct that by replacing the mid-ground leaves with the in-focus leaves from Image 2 (**Figures 2.05a** and **2.05b**).

NOTE: The optical rule for depth of field is that the area of sharp focus extends one-third in front of and two-thirds behind the point of focus.

1. Turn off visibility of all but the BASE IMAGE and MID LEAVES layers. Make the MID LEAVES layer (the one with the middle leaves in focus) active. Lower its opacity to 50% (**Figure 2.5c**).

FIGURE 2.5C

FIGURE 2.5D

FIGURE 2.5E

2. Zoom into the central area of the image, select the Move tool (V), and use the arrow key to move the MID LEAVES layer until it lines up with the background image. Having the top layer at 50% opacity makes it easier to see the layer underneath when aligning the two (**Figures 2.5d** and **2.5e**).

3. Bring the layer's opacity back to 100% and fit the image to the screen (Ctrl/Cmd-0).

4. Option/Alt-click the Add Layer Mask button to create a layer mask filled with black. This allows the background layer to be completely visible. Select a soft 400-pixel brush at 100% opacity, and paint with white on the layer mask over the blurry leaves in the lower-left corner of the image (**Figures 2.5f** and **2.5g**).

NOTE: Remember that with adjustment layers and layer masks, black hides the source layer, while white allows the source layer to be visible. Painting with different opacities shows varying levels of the effect.

FIGURE 2.5F

FIGURE 2.5G

FIGURE 2.6A *Guide lines around the in-focus leaf.*

Step 4: Swapping the Foreground Leaf

The next step is to replace the base image's out-of-focus foreground leaf with the in-focus leaf from the FG LEAF layer. Repeat Step 3, but with one extra step. When you change the focus point of an image, you also change that image's perspective, and that will need to be corrected.

1. First, drag guide lines to the left and right of the leaf, to the upper parts of the leaf, and to its tip (**Figure 2.6a**).

2. Turn off visibility of all layers but the BASE IMAGE 1 and FG LEAF layer. Make the FG LEAF layer the active layer, and select the foreground leaf with the Marquee tool (**Figure 2.6b**).

3. Copy the selection to its own layer (Ctrl/Cmd-J), name this layer FG LEAF PART, and turn off visibility of the FG LEAF source layer. Lower the new layer's opacity to 50% and switch to the Move tool (V). Drag the leaf so that its tip is aligned with the tip of the same leaf on the layer underneath (**Figure 2.6c**).

FIGURE 2.6B *Selecting the sharp foreground leaf.*

FIGURE 2.6C

FIGURE 2.6D

FIGURE 2.6E

4. Using Free Transform (Ctrl/Cmd-T), you are going to shrink the leaf so that it matches the leaf underneath it. First, move the anchor point from the center to the tip of the leaf. That way, everything you do will be in relation to that point, the part of the base image that is in sharpest focus (**Figure 2.6d**).

5. Move the anchor points along the sides and corners until the leaf more or less matches up with the guides.

6. Ctrl/Cmd-click one of the corners of the image. (This is the keyboard shortcut for the Distort tool.) Move each of the corners until the leaf tips are as close to matching as you can get them (**Figure 2.6e**).

7. Right-click the leaf that is bounded by the Free Transform box. (On a Mac, hold the Command key and click the mouse. That's the same as right-clicking in Windows, and produces the same menu choices.) This will bring up the Free Transform menu. In CS2, select Warp (**Figure 2.6f**).

NOTE: Warp is new in CS2. Ben Willmore, in his book, *Photoshop CS2: Up to Speed* (Peachpit, 2005) writes: "The new Warp feature allows you to bend and distort images almost as if they were printed on Silly Putty."

FIGURE 2.6F

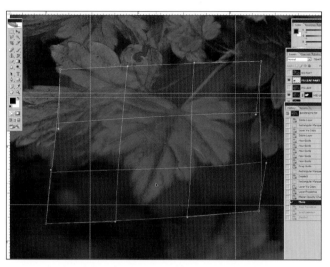

FIGURE 2.6G *Warping the leaf into position.*

8. With CS2's Warp tool, move the image until the tips of the leaves match exactly (**Figure 2.6g**).

9. Click the Hand tool in the Tools palette, then click Apply to complete the transformation. Bring the layer's opacity back to 100% (**Figure 2.6h**).

10. Add a layer mask filled with black. Using a soft 200-pixel brush with white as the foreground color, paint in the area of the leaf you just sized and warped (**Figure 2.6i**).

NOTE: For another description of matching and aligning two images, see "The Registration Problem" in Step 5 of Chapter 3.

FIGURE 2.6H

FIGURE 2.6I

Figure 2.7a *Before.*

Figure 2.7b *After.*

Step 5: Matching the Base and Image 4 Colors

You are going to use the BG PARTS layer to put some image structure elements in the upper-right corner of the background. But the leaves in BG PARTS look bluer than the ones in BASE IMAGE, so you must first match the colors of the two layers.

NOTE: The colors in the images are very subtle. I suggest you open the Histogram palette, set it to All Channels View, and see what happens when you repeatedly click the visibility icon for this layer.

1. Make the BG PARTS layer active, and select Image > Adjustments > Match Color (in Photoshop CS and above).

2. In the Match Color palette, select GREEN FAIRY 16BIT.psd from the Source menu, and select BASE IMAGE from the Layer menu. Click OK (**Figures 2.7a** and **2.7b**).

Step 6: Adding the Background from Image 4

In the final step of the assembly, you will use some of the background details from the BG PARTS layer.

1. Using the Marquee tool (M), select the leaf in the upper-right corner. Copy the selection to its own layer (Ctrl/Cmd-J) (**Figure 2.8a**).

Figure 2.8a *Leaf selected in the BG PARTS layer.*

FIGURE 2.8B

FIGURE 2.8C

2. Turn off the BG PARTS layer, choose the Move tool (V), and drag the new layer up and to the left. Name the new layer BG LEAF (**Figure 2.8b**).

3. Make the BG PARTS layer visible again, move it to the top of the layer stack, then hold down the Alt/Option key, and click the Add Layer Mask button. Select a soft 175-pixel brush and paint in the upper-right corner of the image with white.

4. Click the BG PARTS layer's thumbnail. Using the Marquee tool, select the upper right-hand corner of the layer. Copy the selection to its own layer and name it BG LEAF (**Figure 2.8c**).

5. Add a black-filled layer mask, making sure the foreground color is white and the background color is black. Select a soft 175-pixel brush, and paint in just the area of the leaf. (Make sure that no hard edges remain after brushing.) This layer will be one of the two main building blocks you will use to fill in the aesthetic details.

6. Duplicate the BG LEAF layer. Move the new layer midway down the right side of the image. Choose Edit > Transform > Rotate and rotate the layer 45 degrees clockwise, then move it slightly to the right. Press Enter/Return to apply the transformation. Name this layer BG LEAF 45 (**Figures 2.8d** and **2.8e**).

You now have the two building blocks you need to construct the background. Remember to bear in mind—and make use of—layer order and different levels of opacity.

7. Duplicate the layer BG LEAF. Move the new layer to the upper-left corner of the BG LEAF layer so that only the bottom half of the leaf is showing. Reduce the opacity to around 80%.

8. Duplicate the BG LEAF 45 layer. Move the new layer to the upper right of the BG LEAF 45 layer. Lower the opacity to 80%. Duplicate this layer and move it to the upper left of BG LEAF 45 and lower the opacity to 50%.

9. Duplicate the layer BG LEAF copy. Move that layer so that the upper-right part of the layer is just below the lower-left part of the layer BG LEAF 45 copy. Lower the opacity to 50%.

FIGURE 2.8D

FIGURE 2.8E

10. Duplicate the BG LEAF layer copy 2. Move the new layer so that the upper right of the duplicated layer is below the lower right of the BG LEAF 45 copy layer. Lower the opacity to 50%.

11. Duplicate the BG LEAF 45 layer. Move the new layer to the upper left of the BG LEAF copy 2 layer so that only the bottom half of the leaf is showing. Lower the opacity to 50%. Duplicate this layer and move it to the upper left of BG LEAF 45 and lower the opacity to 50%.

The composite image is now complete. The focal points on the various leaves are all correct, and the upper-right corner has the desired background detail (**Figures 2.8f** and **2.8g**).

FIGURE 2.8F *Before.*

FIGURE 2.8G *After.*

Before starting the next set of aesthetic corrections, you will merge all active layers into one layer while keeping all the previous layers intact. I call this doing "The Move."

1. Click the top layer to make it active.

2. What you do next depends on which version of Photoshop you have. For CS2 and above, press and hold Ctrl-Alt-Shift-E/Cmd-Option-Shift-E. For CS and below, press Ctrl-Alt-Shift/Cmd-Option-Shift, then type N and then E.

In both cases, the result is a master layer that contains all the previous layers. Name it MASTER 1 (**Figure 2.8h**).

NOTE: When you do "The Move" in CS2, the name "Merge Stamp Visible" appears in the History palette.

FIGURE 2.8H *MASTER 1.*

Step 7: Removing the DSLR Sensor Color Cast

You will now deal with the image's color cast attributable to the DSLR sensor. This color cast is caused by data interpolation errors of the CCD or CMOS imager's Bayer array data in the post processing of the capture, and occurs in all digitally captured images.

1. Create a Threshold adjustment layer. Move the slider all the way to the left. Now, slowly move the slider to the right until you see "meaningful" black. You are not looking for the first black pixel, but the black pixels in which you can first make out a shape or shapes. Drop a sample point in the area of meaningful black. You do this by Shift-clicking the desired spot.

NOTE: You were looking for "meaningful" black when finding the black point. But for the white point, you want to get as close as you can to the first white pixel. If you have an image in which the whites are blown out or they are at a value of 255, pick the first pixel that is below that value.

2. Move the Threshold slider all the way to the right, then move it slowly to the left until you see the first or second white pixel. Shift-click a sample point. Click Cancel.

3. Zoom into the area where you placed the first sample point. Create a Curves adjustment layer. With the black eyedropper, click the sample point and click OK. Name this layer BP.

NOTE: Remember to set the black eyedropper in the black point Curves adjustment layer to R:7 B:7 G:7 and the white eyedropper in the white point Curves adjustment layer to R:247 B:247 G:247. You set these values by double-clicking the eyedropper.

4. Do "The Move" and name this layer MASTER 2.

FIGURE 2.9 *The aesthetic choices image map.*

Step 8: Creating the Image Map

Now that you have one image with which to work, it's time to map out what you are going to do to it. When I shot this image, I pre-visualized it as I wanted it to become. Next I asked myself what I might need to create the image that I saw in my mind's eye. I shot, or harvested, images the way I did so that when I sat down at the computer to work, I already had a vision in mind. As I have previously discussed, there is a very specific way the eye sees. In effect, there are two "eyes" involved when it comes to viewing an image: the unconscious eye (the optical, organic sensing device that we call the human eye) and the conscious eye. I will discuss both of these in the next chapter. For now, let's simply apply what you learned in the first chapter.

Here, the choices to be made are all about where and how the viewer's eye will move across the image. In this picture, you want the eye to go first to the top leaf, then to the leaf in the middle, then to the foreground leaf, then to the back set of leaves, and finally, to the background.

NOTE: I suggest you try mapping some of your own images. Start practicing at practicing. When making an image map, keep in mind that it can be fairly loose. What you are doing is setting up a rough game plan (global to granular); you're just making notes of the direction you want to take. The percentages that you decide to use for your finished product may differ from those that you indicate on the image map. These are merely reference points to the ratios and relationships you want in your image.

Select the Pen tool, make the brush size 8 pixels, and choose a yellow color from the color picker. Create a new layer and name it GF OVER ALL IM.

Here is the image map that I created (**Figure 2.9**).

FIGURE 2.10A *Before.*

FIGURE 2.10B *After.*

Step 9: Removing the Blue Cast

Objects photographed in sunlight tend to have a blue cast, and if they are in shadow, they are even bluer (**Figure 2.10a**). You will use the Nik Color Efex Pro 2.0 Skylight Filter to color correct the *Green Fairy* image. This filter removes the blue cast and makes the colors more realistic (**Figures 2.10b** and **2.10c**).

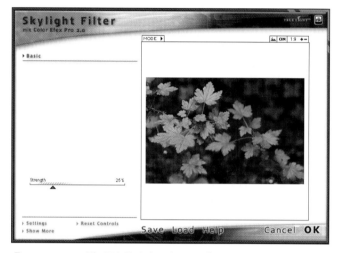

FIGURE 2.10C *The Nik Skylight Filter interface.*

Selective Contrast and Selective Sharpening

As I discussed, the eye goes first to patterns it recognizes in light areas and then in dark ones. The eye also tracks from high to low contrast, in-focus to blur, high to low sharpness (which is different than in-focus to blur), and then, high to low saturation of color. In this next step, you are going to play with contrast and sharpness. But before we begin, let me first define these two terms.

Contrast is often confused with contrast ratio. *Contrast* is the difference in brightness between the light and dark areas of a picture. If there is a large difference between the light and dark areas, the result is an image with high contrast. *Contrast ratio* is the ratio of the lumens, as measured on a meter, of the lightest area in the scene to the darkest area in the scene. By adjusting that ratio, you increase or decrease the contrast in an image.

Sharpening (or specifically in Photoshop, Unsharp masking) is the increasing of the apparent edge contrast by increasing contrast on either side of the pixels' edges. In this way, contrast and sharpness are related. It's worth noting, however, that contrast is normally spoken of on a global scale, and

sharpness is highly localized. When an image is sharpened using Unsharp Masking, nothing is actually being sharpened. What is created is a visually appealing artifact that gives an illusion of sharpness.

NOTE: The technique of Unsharp Masking is an old darkroom printing technique developed in the 1930s. Its actual name is the Craik-O'Brien-Cornsweet Edge illusion, or the Cornsweet edge for short. According to the *Journal of Neuroscience*, **a Cornsweet edge is created "by increasing the apparent edge contrast of an image by adjusting through a blurred copy of the image." Hence the term "unsharpening."**

Though contrast and sharpness, or more specifically, "unsharpness," are technically very similar, they differ in the way they can interact with each other in an image. This is why you will be addressing the issues of selective aesthetic contrast and sharpness on two different layers. Let's start with selective contrast.

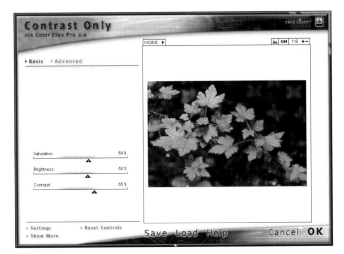

FIGURE 2.10D *The Contrast Only settings.*

Step 10: Selective Contrast
Approach 1. Using the Nik Contrast Only filter

1. Duplicate the SKYLIGHT layer two times. Make the layer SKYLIGHT copy 2 active and rename it CONTRAST.

2. Choose Filter > Nik Color Efex Pro 2.0: traditional filters and select the Contrast Only filter. Start by adjusting the contrast. Move the Contrast slider to the right until the image starts to posterize and the shadows block up, then back the slider down until you're on the fine edge between posterizing and not posterizing. For this image, it happens at the right edge of the yellow zone on the Contrast slider, or 65%. Now move the Brightness slider until the image opens up again, or for this image, 58%. Lastly, adjust the Saturation slider to about 59% (**Figure 2.10d**).

3. Click Advanced in the Contrast Only dialog. To protect the image's shadows and highlights, you must tell the filter where to stop boosting contrast. Move both sliders to the right, then slowly move them to the left until the overall desired amount of contrast is achieved. (Clicking the image in the dialog lets you see the before-and-after effect.) For this image, set the cutoff at 43% for the highlights and 69% for the shadows. Click OK (**Figure 2.10e**).

NOTE: This is obviously too much contrast, but it's usually easier to reduce an effect than to boost it. When using layer masks, it's also better to be a little over than a little under. You can always lower the opacity of the effect, either by using the Fade command on the Edit menu or by lowering the opacity of the layer after you have created the relationship you like.

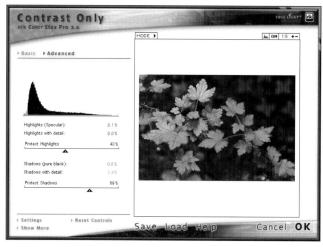

FIGURE 2.10E *The Advanced panel choices.*

4. Create a layer mask and fill it with black. Turn the GF OVERALL IM layer eyeball on. (Make sure that CONTRAST is the active layer, and that the layer mask is active.) Following the image map, do the brushwork (**Figures 2.10f**, **2.10g**, and **2.10h**).

FIGURE 2.10F *Before.*

FIGURE 2.10G *After global contrast.*

FIGURE 2.10H *After selective contrast.*

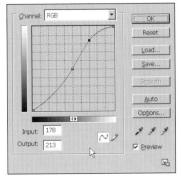

FIGURE 2.11A

Approach 2. Without the Nik Contrast filter

What follows is the classic way to create a contrast curve that, unlike the Brightness/Contrast adjustment in Photoshop, minimizes the creation of artifacts.

1. Create a Curves adjustment layer. Click the center point of the curve to lock it. Place the mouse pointer over the curve, two grid lines up and right. Drag that point up and to the left to increase the contrast to a level that is visually pleasing. Don't drag too far; you just need a small amount. Click OK. Name the layer CONTRAST (**Figure 2.11a**).

2. Create a layer mask filled with black, and do the appropriate brushwork.

NOTE: This can also be done with the Brightness/Contrast sliders: Image > Adjustments > Brightness/Contrast. (In my opinion the Nik software algorithm is superior to the one in Photoshop.)

Step 11: Selective Sharpening

Some people believe that you should only sharpen an image to allow for an increased output size. Others believe that sharpening is the last thing you do before printing. I believe neither is true. Moreover, most people don't know how to correctly sharpen an image once, let alone how to correctly sharpen an image multiple times.

Whether TIFF, JPEG, or RAW, all digitally captured files require some form of sharpening. This is due to the interpolation process that occurs when the data is converted from its original form to the form on which you will work.

In addition to sharpening the original digital capture, another consideration is *aesthetic*, or *selective* sharpening, which you are going to do in this step. And of course, there is sharpening for output, which is one of the last things you will do to an image, but not always the last. So an image may be sharpened as many as three times.

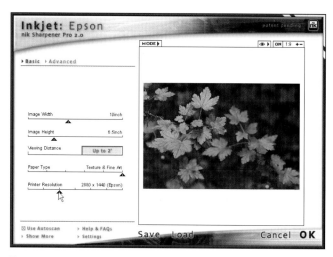

FIGURE 2.11B

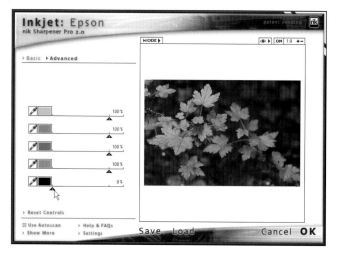

FIGURE 2.11C

The key is understanding what sharpening is. As I discussed at the beginning of this section, Unsharp Masking doesn't really sharpen an image. It adds visually appealing artifacts that create the illusion of increased sharpness. There are also other issues at play. When you view an image on your monitor you are viewing a file that is 240- to 360-ppi image on a 72-dpi screen. Such images will be printed at either 720, 1440, 2880, or 5760 dpi. So what looks right on the screen is probably under-sharpened for output, and what looks over-sharpened on the screen is probably about right. How do you know how much to over-sharpen? You don't—and that's the problem.

There's more: flat planes, linear lines, foliage, blur, and skin tones all need to be sharpened differently. In addition, viewing distance, paper type, printer output resolution, printer type, and the amount of dot gain (the expansion of the ink droplet on the paper) are all factors when it comes to sharpening. Because of this, I sharpen using Approach 1 below. The Nik software is able to detect if something has been sharpened more than once and adjusts accordingly.

Approach 1. Using the Nik Sharpener Pro 2.0 filter

1. Turn off the CONTRAST layer and make the SHARPEN layer the active layer. Zoom in on the leaf that is the main focus of this image.

2. Go to Filter > Nik Sharpener Pro 2.0. Choose the appropriate printer output. In my case, that is > Inkjet: Epson. Leave the viewing distance set to Auto and the paper dimensions to what comes up in the dialog. You are creating a fine-art print, so move the Paper Type slider to the left and select Texture & Fine Art. I normally use Epson Somerset Velvet or Epson Textured Fine Art paper. The printer resolution for this paper is 2880 × 1440 (**Figure 2.11b**).

The Advance pane of the dialog has a series of color boxes and eyedroppers. The eyedroppers are for sampling the colors with which you want to work. Using the Nik plug-in, you can pick the colors you want to sharpen, as well as the colors you *don't* want to sharpen. In other words, you define the amount of sharpness for each color you sample, starting with the greens.

FIGURE 2.11D *Before.*

FIGURE 2.11E *After.*

FIGURE 2.11F

3. Click the top eyedropper and sample any part of the upper green leaf on which you are zoomed in. Then, click in the middle leaf area, then on the foreground leaf, then on the back leaves to the lower right, and last, on the darkest part of the background. Move the slider to 0%. In this sharpening layer, you want to sharpen just the greens, not the blacks. Click OK. Now select the blending mode Luminosity. Even though we just sharpened *by* color, we don't necessarily want to sharpen *the* colors (**Figures 2.11c**, **2.11d**, and **2.11e**).

4. Ctrl/Cmd-click the layer mask part of the CONTRAST layer. You should see marching ants on the image.

5. Make SHARPEN the active layer and create a layer mask. It should look just like the layer mask you made on the CONTRAST layer. Turn on the CONTRAST layer, move the SHARPEN layer above it, and lower the SHARPEN layer until the relationship between sharpness and contrast appeals to you. For me, it was at 75% (**Figure 2.11f**).

Approach 2. Using the Unsharp Mask Filter in Photoshop

If you don't have the Nik Sharpener Pro 2.0 filter, you can use the Unsharp Mask filter, but that's something I suggest only as a last resort. Not that it's a bad piece of coding, but there are better and more intuitive ways to sharpen an image. The best way is in the LAB color space, sharpening the Lightness channel and not the A and B channels.

To sharpen in the LAB space requires converting the file from the RGB space to the LAB space.

NOTE: I learned this sharpening technique and the approach to increasing saturation in Step 13 from Dan Margulis. I highly recommend his book *Photoshop LAB Color: The Canyon Conundrum and Other Adventures in the Most Powerful Colorspace* (Peachpit, 2005).

Method A: Using Unsharp Mask

1. Make the SHARPEN layer active.

2. Do a "Save as" in the File Save Option dialog box and click the layers off. Name the file SHARPEN.psd.

NOTE: The reason you save the file as a .psd, rather than a Tiff, is that non-layered .psd files are smaller than non-layered Tiff files.

3. Open the newly saved file and choose Image > Mode > Lab Color. In the Channels palette, make the Lightness channel active. Keep the other two channels visible because you want to judge the quality of the sharpening on a color image, not on a black-and-white one.

4. Sharpen the image using the Unsharp Mask filter.

5. Open the Layers palette. Select the Move tool and click the Background layer. Holding the Shift key down, drag it to the master file on which you have been working. Name the newly imported layer SHARPEN.

6. Do steps 4 and 5 of Approach 1. Close the SHARPEN.psd.

Method B: Creating an Action

Many of the limitations of sharpening have to do with the lighter artifacts it inserts, rather than the darker ones. The following action separates the two functions; the darkening is on the middle layer and the lightening on top, and the action automatically cuts the lightening in half.

1. Create the following Action. Start with a duplicate copy of your base image, with only the desired layers visible.

START ACTION

   1) Layer: Merge Visible

   2) Mode: Lab Color

   3) Make TWO duplicate layers

   4) Change mode of top layer to Luminosity

   5) Filter: Sharpen > Unsharp Mask

PAUSE ACTION

NOTE: You are working on the L channel only, even though it is not explicitly selected, since Luminosity mode excludes the A and B (more about A and B channels in a little bit). Now, over-sharpen this image. (By "over-sharpen" I don't mean "make it look ridiculous." I mean "Go a bit further than you know is right.")

   6) Click OK to RESUME ACTION.

   7) Merge the top two layers only, leaving the newly merged top (over sharpened) layer in Normal mode.

   8) Mode: RGB; Flatten image? =NO.

   9) Duplicate the top layer. (You now have one original and two, over-sharpened layers.)

  10) Change the opacity of the top layer to 50%.

  11) Change the mode of the MIDDLE layer to Darken.

END ACTION.

2. If you're lucky, what you've just done will give you a nice result. If not, adjust the opacities of the middle and the top layers to change lightening and darkening independently. When you are satisfied, flatten the image and put it back into your original file. (Remember to Shift-drag when placing it in the original file.)

3. Name the layer SHARPEN and do steps 4 and 5 of Approach 1.

Step 12: Using Curves for Selective Light to Dark

1. Ctrl/Cmd-click the SHARPEN layer's layer mask. Go to Select > Inverse (Shift-Ctrl-I/Shift-Cmd-I). You are inverting the mask you created earlier. You want to darken the background and not the leaves.

2. Create a Curves adjustment layer.

NOTE: To get a small grid, Alt/Option-click the center of the dialog.

3. Click the center of the diagonal line and drag the curve line down and right. For this image, it was one square down. Click OK. Be sure to select the blending mode Luminosity. (You don't want to change the color or increase the saturation, just darken the color.) Name this layer L2D LUM (for light to dark luminosity) (**Figures 2.12a, 2.12b,** and **2.12c**).

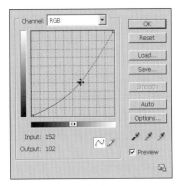

FIGURE 2.12A *Using the Curves adjustment layer.*

FIGURE 2.12B *Before.*

FIGURE 2.12C *After.*

Step 13: Increasing Saturation in the LAB Color Space

1. Save the file. Next, "Save As" in the File Save Option dialog and click the layers off. Name the file GREEN FAIRY LAB.psd.

2. Open the file GREEN FAIRY LAB.psd. Go to Image > Mode and select Lab Color. You have just converted the file to the LAB Color space.

3. Create a Curves adjustment layer. Select "a." and move both the top and bottom anchor points over two grid lines (**Figures 2.13a**, **2.13b**, **2.13c**, and **2.13d**).

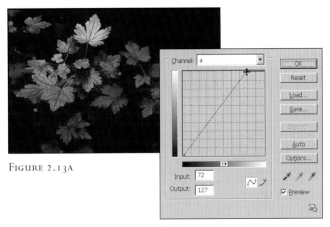

FIGURE 2.13A

FIGURE 2.13B

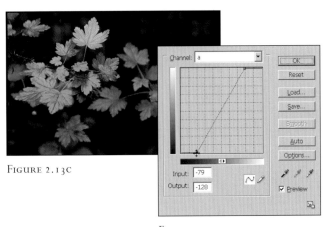

FIGURE 2.13C

FIGURE 2.13D

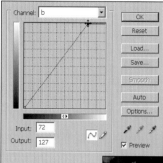

FIGURE 2.13E

FIGURE 2.13F

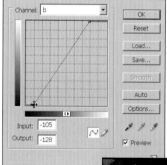

FIGURE 2.13G

FIGURE 2.13H

4. Now Select "b." Move the top anchor point over two grid lines and the bottom over one grid line (**Figures 2.13e, 2.13f, 2.13g,** and **2.13h**).

NOTE: The "L" of LAB is the Lightness or Luminance channel; "A" is Green to Magenta, and "B" is Blue to Yellow. Keep in mind that the settings used here are only for this image. As a rule, I never move the anchor points more than three grid points to the left or right, depending on whether it's to the top or bottom of the curve. As much as possible, I try to keep movement to one grid point.

5. Make a Master layer and do "The Move." Save the file as GREEN FAIRY LAB.psd.

6. Shift-drag the Master layer onto the GREEN FAIRY.psd file. Name this layer LAB.

7. Ctrl/Cmd-click the layer mask of the CONTRAST layer and create a layer mask on the LAB layer (**Figures 2.13i** and **2.13j**).

8. Save the file.

FIGURE 2.13I

FIGURE 2.13J

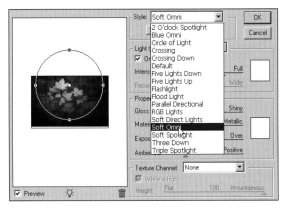

FIGURE 2.14A

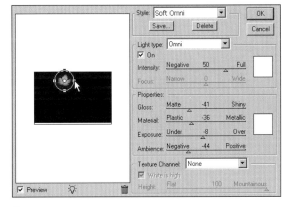

FIGURE 2.14B

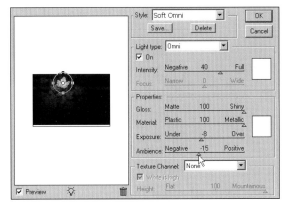

FIGURE 2.14C *Settings in the Lighting Effects dialog.*

Step 14: Adding a Ray of Sunlight

To add the final touch to this image, you can create the effect of a ray of sunlight hitting the various leaves. But first, there is one problem you need to address. The file on which you are working is in 16-bit, and the Render > Lighting Effects filter works only in 8-bit.

1. "Save as" in the File Save Option dialog and click the layers off. Name the file GREEN FAIRY LIGHTING 8BIT.psd.

2. Open the file GREEN FAIRY LIGHTING 8BIT.psd.

3. Shift-drag the Curves adjustment layer L2D LUM from the GREEN FAIRY 16bit.psd. Turn this layer off.

4. Convert the file to 8-bit.

5. Duplicate the Background layer. (Photoshop may have named it layer 1, depending on which version you have.)

6. Select Filter > Render > Lighting Effects.

7. In the Style menu, select Soft Omni. Move the center point of the light onto the upper leaf, which is the image's primary focus area. Reduce the size of the light circle to the size of the leaf (**Figures 2.14a** and **2.14b**).

8. Under Properties, increase Ambience to –15, Exposure to –8, Material to Metallic, and Gloss to Shiny. Set Intensity at 40 (**Figure 2.14c**).

NOTE: With the Lighting Effects filter, it's easier to make menu choices from bottom to top.

9. Create a second light by clicking and dragging the light-bulb icon to the point on the preview that you want to highlight, in this case, the center of the middle leaves. Align the center dot under the center dot of the top leaf. From the Light type menu, select Omni. Set the intensity at 13.

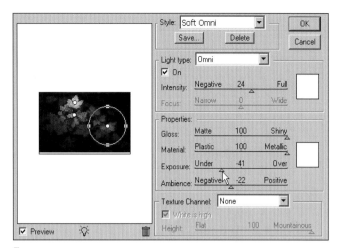

FIGURE 2.14D

FIGURE 2.14E

10. Create a third light, placing the center point in the middle of the group of leaves at the right side of the image. Again, select Soft Omni, lower the intensity to 24, adjust Exposure to –41 and Ambience to –22, and Click OK. Name this layer LIGHTING (**Figure 2.14d**).

NOTE: The reason for adjusting the exposure and ambience both at the beginning and the end of using the Render > Lighting Effects filter is that the first adjustment is global and the second is granular. Before you did the final fine-tuning, the upper leaf was completely blown out.

11. Lower the intensity of the LIGHTING layer to 75%.

12. Turn on and make active the L2D LUM Curves adjustment layer, and lower the opacity till it is visually appealing, which for this image is 25%.

13. Do "The Move." Name this layer MASTER FINAL. The image is now ready to be saved, scaled, sharpened for final output, and printed (**Figure 2.14e**).

Expanding Your Vision

I am always doing things I can't do; that's how I get to do them.

—Pablo Picasso

Image harvesting is a way to recreate what you originally saw (in spite of the limitations of camera technology) and at the same time, use the camera's limitations so as to produce an aesthetically pleasing result. So is this image a believable improbability or a believable probability? Is your answer the same as it was at the beginning of this lesson? If your opinion has changed, you will realize that your feeling for any image may change as you work with it, and that's okay as long as it suits your vision and retains your voice.

In the next chapter, you will further explore the concept of image harvesting. The goal will be not only to recreate your original vision, but to cause shape to become the unwitting ally of color in the pursuit of deliberately guiding the viewer's unconscious eye.

Shibumi[2]

Untitled

American Gothic

American Beauty

Seattle Sequence[1]

W.B.

It's All a Matter of Perspective

Flowers are Nature's Way of Laughing[2]

Welcome to Oz[1]

A Sock Then a Shoe: Norman Lear

If I Were a Raindrop

Every Woods Has a Whisper

FIGURE 3.1

FIGURE 3.2 *Transforming the Cades Cove flowers.*

Chapter 3

The Unwitting Ally

Light, gesture, and color are the key components of any photograph.
Light and color are obvious, but it is gesture that is the most important.
There is gesture in everything. It's up to you to find the gesture that is most telling.

—Jay Maisel

In this chapter, you will apply the image-harvesting concept to the image-editing process in order to support the aesthetic choices you make regarding light, shape, gesture, and color when you first take the picture. Picasso said, "Art is the lie that tells the truth." With that in mind, you will also apply techniques to create an aesthetically satisfying final image rather than a "historically" accurate one. Finally, you will use the approach introduced in Chapter 1, and expanded in Chapter 2, to guide the viewer's unconscious eye through the image.

The concepts behind this lesson are the outcome of conversations that I've had over the years with two great photographers: Jay Maisel, who has forgotten more than I will ever know about light, gesture, and color, and who first introduced me to the concept; and my uncle, photographer CJ Elfont, who taught me photography and, most importantly, how the eye "sees." When you master this lesson, you will have grasped the heart of what I have discovered about how it all works. The real journey begins now.

On Light, Color, Shape, and Gesture

The late painter and designer Josef Albers said that "shape is the enemy of color." By that he meant that when shape is in the presence of color, we tend to remember the shape and not the color. In this sense, shape isn't necessarily a friend to color. But if you understand how to control color—regardless of whether the photograph is color or black and white—you will have complete mastery of the images you create. The key is to find a way to cause shape to become color's unwitting ally, and thereby make color a "shape" that the viewer will remember.

This is easier said than done, of course. What you need is a catalyst to make shape and color work in harmony. And this is where pattern comes in.

Patterns are shapes we tend to see in things, sometimes when they aren't really there. Patterns tend to manifest themselves as shapes. Whether it's light coming through tree leaves, a paper bag in a subway trash can, or raindrops on a windshield, everything can form or be perceived as a pattern. Patterns are interesting, but a pattern *interrupted* is more interesting. If you interrupt the pattern, you are on the path to finding a way to using shape as the unwitting ally of color.

As Jay Maisel says, light and color are obvious, but it is gesture that is most important. In the photograph of my niece, the gesture is obvious. The pattern we recognize first is her face, and the finger stuck in her nose interrupts that pattern (**Figure 3.3**).

Let's look at an example of an image where gesture is not as plain as the nose on my niece's face. Look at the image of the flower and the leaves, then look away (**Figure 3.4**). Which color do you remember? Most people would say magenta, purple, or red. Even though 90% of the image is made up of greens, we tend to remember the part with the most shape. The shape has become an unwitting ally of the color. The color is further reinforced because the magenta flower's shape

FIGURE 3.3 *A universal gesture.*

FIGURE 3.4 *Do you see the green or the magenta?*

and circular pattern is interrupted by the linear pattern of the green blades. Further, the magenta flower appears to be moving away from the green blades, and this pattern holds the gesture that is most telling.

Of light, gesture, and color, light is the most frequently taken for granted. We see it, it's there, end of story. But rather than merely accepting its presence, why not consider viewing it as an object? Treat it as if it were a solid and a part of the experience being expressed in the photograph.

Take, for example, these images from the "Seattle Sequence" series. The light tells the story of the moment in each image, whether black and white or color. (If you can see something, it has color. The artist Matisse said, "Black is the queen of all colors.")

NOTE: The 12 images that are the Seattle Sequence were shot in 45 minutes. My skill as a photographer had nothing to do with how quickly I shot; I had forgotten to charge the battery. I saw the charge eroding as I watched one of the prettiest displays of light that I have ever seen. Shafts of light broke through a departing rainstorm while a new rainstorm was moving in. Knowing that I had little time to record these images, fear became my caffeine, and I shot until my battery died. Among the images that came from those 45 minutes were 12 that I thought were particularly outstanding. The lessons that I learned were to just shoot the image, don't think about shooting the image, and carry an extra battery.

In each instance, no matter how brief, I perceived the image in its final form as I photographed it, and that perception determined how I harvested the images. In each one, the light informs the image, makes the patterns and interrupts them. In each instance, light is as physical and tangible a thing as the flowers. What is at play here is the use of positive and negative space as well as dark and light isolates (**Figures 3.5a, 3.5b, 3.5c, 3.6a, 3.6b,** and **3.6c**).

FIGURE 3.5A

FIGURE 3.5B

FIGURE 3.6A

FIGURE 3.6B

FIGURE 3.5C

FIGURE 3.6C *Seattle Sequence: Image 3.*

Varying Positive and Negative Space

In the next image of calla lilies, the light isolates are the two flowers that are slightly to the right of center. The gesture that is most telling is the spiral that starts from the upper right in the dark isolate. This is the darkest area in which there are definable structures, and it continues to the center of the photograph, where there is a light isolate. This particular pattern occurred by happenstance, but I reinforced it by varying the use of positive and negative space, which often occupies the same spaces as dark and light isolates (**Figures 3.7a**, **3.7b**, and **3.7c**).

FIGURE 3.7A   FIGURE 3.7B

FIGURE 3.7C *Seattle Sequence: Image 8.*

The Isolate Theory (*A very brief version*)

The Isolate Theory, conceived by CJ Elfont, explains the interrelationship of the elements (or isolates) in a photograph. Properly used, they result in effective composition; i.e., one that communicates the photographer's vision to his or her audience. The primary isolate is the first element (either light or dark) in the composition to which the eye is drawn. Supporting isolates are different in density from the primary one, but they complement and enhance it. When the supporting isolates flow within the composition and support the primary isolate without conflicting with it, you get the viewer's attention and communication happens. Here's an example. If two dark isolate buildings are separated in a field of intermediate isolates, the eye has no focal point on which to start. But if three dark buildings are positioned closer together at an angle or in an S-curve or C-curve, then a flow occurs. That flow allows for a gradual appreciation of the buildings alone, as well as their relationship to one another, without dividing interest and interrupting the feeling that the buildings belong together and have something to say as a group.

By varying the levels of positive and negative space, and by using selective contrast and sharpness, I gradually created the dramatic effect of motion in a still image. I also interrupted the pattern of the background with the spiral of light-to-dark, and in this way found the most telling gesture. All of this was already present in the image, but it had to be brought out. Like Michelangelo, who claimed that he simply removed everything that wasn't his sculpture from the stone, I removed everything that wasn't my vision of the image from the file.

If gesture is the expression of the photograph, and light is its language, then colors are its words, and contrast, saturation, and sharpness are the alphabet. Without words, language and expression have no meaning. Without the alphabet, there are no words.

If the words of color are lost in a cacophony of shapes, the image will be less than it could be. The better you support color and its expression, the better your images will be appreciated. And just as in a street fight, the only rule is that there are no rules. All elements are available for you to use and exploit. Everything you do is in service of the print, which will always be in service of what is ultimately the most important: your voice and vision.

Cades Cove Moving Light

I shot this series of images one morning at sunrise in Cades Cove (in the Great Smoky Mountains National Park). Without planning what I would shoot, I had gotten up extraordinarily early hoping to shoot some "stuff" in the fog at sunrise. I actually saw the field of flowers after all the fog had burned off and I was about to leave. I just found the images, or maybe they found me.

As I crawled around on my hands and knees among the flowers in the dew, the light moved and changed. I tried to approach the light the same way I approached the flowers, as if it were a solid object. I made sure to get as many captures with as many options as I could. Moments like the ones photographed there happen; you can't make them re-happen.

If you look at the images I shot, you can see an evolution of visions as I experienced the flowers. It is in that journey that I discovered the destination (**Figure 3.8**).

FIGURE 3.8 *The Cades Cove contact sheet.*

Creating a Single Image

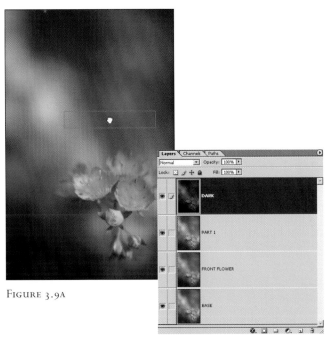

Figure 3.9a

Figure 3.9b *The layers in the Layers palette.*

Figure 3.9c *A close-up of the flowers before any manipulation.*

Step 1: Assembling the Base Image

As you have done in the previous chapters, you are going to approach the creation of this image going from global to granular. The following steps will lead you through how I removed everything that was not my vision from the Cades Cove flower images, so I could achieve my previsualized composition.

1. Open these four files:

   smoky DLWS0655BASE.tif

   smoky DLWS0653 FRONT FLOWER.tif

   smoky DLWS0654PART1.tif

   smoky DLWS0656DARK.tif

2. Starting with the file smoky DLWS0653 FRONT FLOWER, click on the icon of the image in the Layers palette. Hold down the Shift key as you drag the image to the destination file, which in this case will be smoky DLWS0655BASE (**Figure 3.9a**). Do the same with smoky DLWS0654PART1 and smoky DLWS0656DARK.

3. After each drag and drop, give the new layer a meaningful name and close each source file. Name the new layers FRONT FLOWER, PART ONE, and DARK. Leave the file's original layer as the Background (**Figure 3.9b**).

4. After moving all the files and creating the master file, choose File > Save As and name it BLUE MASTER FLOWER 16BIT. Be sure to save it as a Photoshop document (.psd) and not as a layered TIFF (**Figure 3.9c**).

FIGURE 3.10A *The initial layer stack.*

FIGURE 3.10B *Sizing the brush to match an element in the image.*

FIGURE 3.10C

FIGURE 3.10D

FIGURE 3.10E *The painted layer mask.*

Now that you have created the master file, you can start to make some structural and aesthetic choices. Here are some initial considerations:

- The focus points are different on the front flower, the main flower, and the back part of the main flower.
- The light hitting the various flowers differs.
- Aesthetically, you will want to support the image's pastel blues and light purples rather than the greens.
- You want the viewer's eye to go from the upper-left flower, to the lower middle, to the middle right, and finally to the back flower.

Step 2: The Front Flower

1. Turn off visibility for the top two layers and duplicate the FRONT FLOWER layer. This will give you a road map of the layer you will be concealing (**Figure 3.10a**).

2. Turn off the layer you just duplicated and make the FRONT FLOWER layer active. Create a layer mask filled with black.

3. At 100% opacity, select a soft brush about the same size as the lower front flower (**Figure 3.10b**).

4. Make sure the foreground color is white, zoom in, and brush out the bottom flower and the right middle flower (**Figures 3.10c** and **3.10d**). The painted area appears on the layer mask (**Figure 3.10e**).

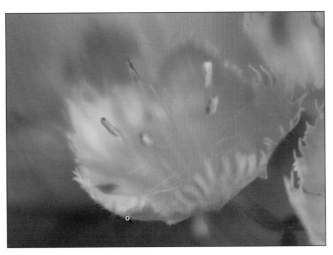

FIGURE 3.10F *Pistils in focus.*

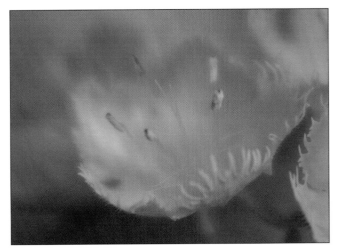

FIGURE 3.10G *Blurry pistils.*

5. Toggle the FRONT FLOWER COPY layer on and off. You see that the front part of the upper-left flower and its two pistils are in sharper focus than the base image, so you are going to use them (**Figures 3.10f** and **3.10g**).

6. Turn the FRONT FLOWER COPY layer off. Make FRONT FLOWER and its layer mask active. Reduce the brush size so it fits into the front part of the flower (a diameter of 70 pixels or so). Paint over the front edge of the flower from the upper right all the way to the lower left. Paint over the two front pistils, too (**Figures 3.10h** and **3.10i**).

7. Go to full frame (Cmd-0/Ctrl-0), and save the file.

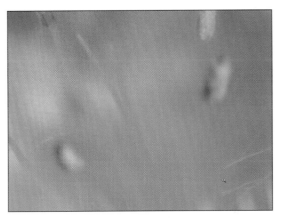

FIGURE 3.10H *Close-up of pistils before sharpening.*

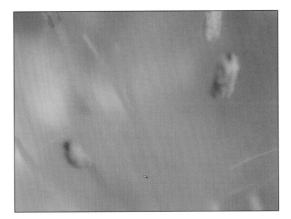

FIGURE 3.10I *The pistils are now much sharper.*

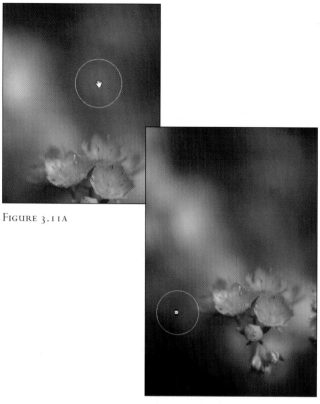

FIGURE 3.11A

FIGURE 3.11B

FIGURE 3.11C *The final layer mask.*

Step 3: The Blurred Background

1. Toggle the FRONT FLOWER COPY layer back on. Notice the difference between this and the BASE layers: the Background of the FRONT FLOWER COPY is darker and blurrier. To support the blue aspect and not the green, you will use aspects of the front flower image to enhance aspects of the base image.

2. Hide the FRONT FLOWER COPY layer again, and select the FRONT FLOWER layer mask. Choose a brush opacity of 50%, increase the brush size to the width of the blurry spot above and slightly to the right of the flowers. Paint over all the green areas. Change to 20% opacity, then brush over the blue part of the background (**Figures 3.11a**, **3.11b**, and **3.11c**).

Step 4: Small Flower Parts

You will now use three aspects of the PART ONE layer: the leaves of the lower flower, the hairs on the inside upper-left flower, and the lighting on the inside of the flower.

1. Duplicate the PART ONE layer and turn off the duplicate. Select the PART ONE layer, make it visible, and add a layer mask filled with black. Select a small, soft brush about 40 pixels in diameter. (You will be working on very small image elements of the layer, and a larger brush might cause registration problems between layers.)

2. Make sure the layer mask is active, and paint with white over the leaves surrounding the lower flower (**Figures 3.12a** and **3.12b**).

3. Brush in the hairs and the area of the flower where the light is different. Turn on the PART ONE copy layer to see if you missed anything (**Figures 3.12c**, **3.12d**, and **3.12e**).

NOTE: The copy layers are used here simply for comparison. When you fill a layer mask with black, working on it can feel like a psychic experience. Having a copy layer to refer to makes the job easier.

4. Toggle the DARK layer on and off. You should see a slight registration problem; the layers don't quite line up. That's because I underexposed the shot by one f-stop, and I lost the image alignment while I was changing the aperture setting.

NOTE: When I'm shooting in image-harvesting mode, I will under- and overexpose shots by one or two f-stops. That way, I can extend the dynamic range of my final images by up to four stops, should I want to. If I later need to darken aspects of an image, I will get a smoother look if it's done in the camera rather than in Photoshop. It's also faster. You're already shooting, and taking one or two more pictures can save you hours of image editing.

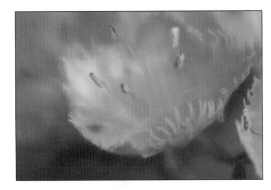

FIGURE 3.12C

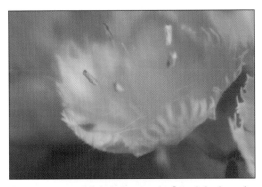

FIGURE 3.12D *Subtly lightening the flower's leading edge.*

FIGURE 3.12A

FIGURE 3.12B *Lightening the small foreground flower.*

FIGURE 3.12E *The PART 1 layer mask.*

FIGURE 3.13A   FIGURE 3.13B *Fixing the registration problem.*

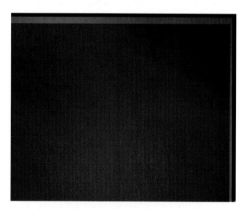

FIGURE 3.13C *With all the layers active.*

FIGURE 3.13D *With just the DARK layer active.*

Step 5: The Registration Problem

Next, fix the registration issue the same way you did in the first image-harvesting lesson. See also "Swap the Foreground Leaf," in Chapter 2.

1. Make the DARK layer active and visible, reduce its opacity to 50%, and zoom into the area of the flowers.

2. Using the Move tool (V) and the arrow keys, move the layer until the flowers line up (**Figures 3.13a** and **3.13b**).

3. Raise the opacity to 100% and toggle the layer on and off. It may appear that you have solved one problem only to create another. By moving the DARK layer down and to the left to line up the flower, you ran out of image at the top and right. The gray-and-white checkerboard shows how far we moved the DARK layer from the actual edge of the image, but it's less serious than the registration problem you just fixed. You can deal with it later (**Figures 3.13c** and **3.13d**).

4. Create a layer mask filled with black. Select a soft brush at 50% opacity and make it approximately the same size as the blurry spot in the center-right of the picture (**Figure 3.13e**).

FIGURE 3.13E *Using an aspect of the image to determine brush size.*

FIGURE 3.13F *The DARK layer mask.*

FIGURE 3.13G

NOTE: I always try to use aspects of the image to define the sizes of the brushes I use.

5. Start by brushing just the green areas. Then go over the blue parts of the background at 20% opacity (**Figure 3.13f**).

6. The relationship between light and dark in the background is visually appealing, but the background itself is now too dark. To fix it, reduce the layer's overall opacity by 47% (**Figure 3.13g**).

Step 6: Creating the First Master Layer

There are several ways you can deal with the issue of the lighter edge (**Figures 3.13h** and **3.13i**). You can crop it, which I don't recommend unless there is no other choice, or you can use the Patch tool, the Healing Brush, or even the Clone Stamp tool. But first, you have to create your first master layer.

Do "The Move" (for CS and below, Ctrl-Alt-Shift-N and Ctrl-Alt-Shift-E/Cmd-Option-Shift-N and Cmd-Option-Shift-E; for CS2 and above, Ctrl-Alt-Shift-E/Cmd-Option-Shift-E). Name this layer MASTER 1 and save the file.

FIGURE 3.13H *Notice that we still have the faint line of lightness on top and down the right of the image.*

FIGURE 3.13I *The lighter edge.*

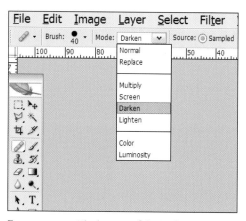

FIGURE 3.13J *The location of the Darken mode in the Option bar.*

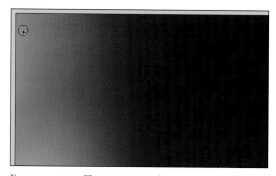

FIGURE 3.13K *The starting sample point.*

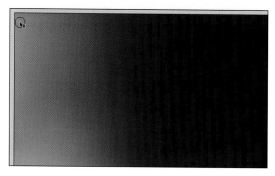

FIGURE 3.13L *Placing the Healing Brush, and what the effect looks like while using the Healing Brush.*

1. Select the Healing Brush tool, or the Clone Stamp tool if you have an older version of Photoshop. Choose Darken from the Mode menu in the Options bar (**Figure 3.13j**). Position the brush slightly under the light strip along the top of the image on which you are about to work. Option-click/Alt-click to define the spot as the source for the pixels you will use to fix the lighter area (**Figures 3.13k** and **3.13l**).

2. Move the Healing Brush up, so that the line between light and dark bisects the brush. Drag it to the right until it reaches the right edge of the image. Repeat the process, going down the right edge of the image from top to bottom (**Figure 3.13m**).

You have now solved the biggest problem with this image, which was making one image on which you could work. You can now move on to making the color correction and aesthetic choices that will make the image sing.

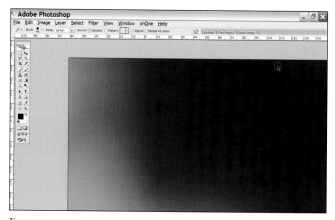

FIGURE 3.13M

Color Corrections and Aesthetic Choices

FIGURE 3.14A *After defining the black point.*

FIGURE 3.14B *The result of defining both the black and white sample points.*

Step 1: Removing Digital Color Cast

The next task is to correct the file's color cast. Use the Threshold adjustment layer approach, as explained in Chapter 1.

NOTE: Remember to set your black eyedropper value to R: 7, B: 7, G: 7 and your white eyedropper value to R: 247, G: 247, B: 247.

1. Press Cmd-0/Ctrl-0 to zoom out, so the entire image is visible in your window.

2. Add a temporary Threshold adjustment layer. While the Threshold dialog is still open, drag the slider to the left to find the image's black point, and to the right to find the white point. Shift-click in each spot to place a Color Sampler. Click Cancel.

3. Create two Curves adjustment layers, one for the light (or white) point and one for the dark (or black) point. In each dialog, click with the appropriate eyedropper on the Color Sampler to define the black and white points (**Figures 3.14a** and **3.14b**).

NOTE: This is a perfect example of why it's a good idea to separate the white and black points into different adjustment layers. There are things about the color I like in the black point correction and others I don't. The same holds true for the white point, as well as for the combination of white and black points. By putting them on separate adjustment layers, I can mask what I don't like.

FIGURE 3.14C *After doing the brushwork on the black point Curves adjustment layer.*

FIGURE 3.14D

FIGURE 3.14G *The image after doing brushwork on both the black and white point Curves adjustment layers.*

FIGURE 3.14E *After doing the brushwork on the white point Curves adjustment layer.*

FIGURE 3.14F

FIGURE 3.14H *The black point Curves layer only.*

FIGURE 3.14I *The white point Curves layer only.*

4. What the black point correction did to the background color looks good, but it also darkened the image's edges too much. Activate the black point Curves adjustment layer's mask. Starting with a brush at 25% opacity, paint with black along the bottom right edge of the image, then set the brush's opacity at 50%, and brush over the lower left area of the image twice. (This is the same as setting the brush opacity to 75%. See the Unmasking Layer Masks sidebar in Chapter One.) With the brush still set at 50% opacity, brush in the upper middle edge area to bring back parts of the original, uncorrected image (**Figures 3.14c** and **3.14d**). Stay at 50% opacity, and, on the white point layer's mask, paint the lower right corner of the image twice, then move to the upper right corner, and paint that area once. Paint the small blue area in the middle of the image and paint the area of purples and light blues from the upper left corner down to the upper flowers. Finally, rebrush the lower part of last area (**Figures 3.14e** and **3.14f**). This is what the image should look like after working on both the black and white point Curves adjustment layers (**Figure 3.14g**).

This is what the image looks like when only the black point Curves layer is activated (**Figure 3.14h**). Here is the image with only the white point Curves layer activated (**Figure 3.14i**).

5. Activate both Curves layers, then do "The Move," name this layer MASTER 2, and save the file.

Step 2: Image Harvesting from Within a Single Image

As I discussed earlier, a pattern is interesting, but a pattern interrupted is more interesting. Currently, the image on which you are working has a pattern of blues and greens in the background. You want to strengthen that pattern while reinforcing the blues over the greens. For that, you need some shapes along the lower-left and upper-right edges of the image that are more blue than green. Paying attention to the direction of the light will determine from where you sample the image.

1. With the Marquee tool (M), make a selection of the upper-left corner (**Figure 3.15a**).

2. Copy the selection to its own layer (Cmd-J/Ctrl-J). Drag the selection to the lower-left corner. Name this layer LOWER CORNER (**Figure 3.15b**).

To make the selection unrecognizable, you'll distort it the same way you did the leaf in the image-harvesting chapter.

3. Select the Free Transform tool. Holding down the Cmd/Ctrl key, put the cursor on the upper-right anchor point. Distort the layer until it looks like this (**Figure 3.15c**).

4. Repeat the process using the upper-left anchor point (**Figure 3.15d**).

FIGURE 3.15A

FIGURE 3.15B

FIGURE 3.15C

FIGURE 3.15D

FIGURE 3.15E

FIGURE 3.15F

FIGURE 3.15G

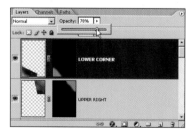

FIGURE 3.15H

FIGURE 3.15I

5. Double-click the middle of the selection. You should have something that looks like this (**Figure 3.15e**).

6. Move the layer so the edge of it is placed as shown here (**Figure 3.15f**).

7. Create a layer mask filled with black. With a 50% opacity brush, paint over the lower-left corner to reveal part of the LOWER CORNER layer. Do the same thing with the upper-right corner.

8. Make the MASTER 2 layer active. With the Marquee tool, select an area of the lower-middle left side of the image (**Figure 3.15g**). Repeat the layer-copying process, and name that layer UPPER RIGHT.

9. Move the selection to the upper-right corner. Repeat Steps 3–5, so the image looks something like this (**Figure 3.15h**).

Double-click inside the layer to accept the transformation. Add a black-filled layer mask and paint with white to reveal the UPPER RIGHT layer.

10. Finally, balance the lower corner so it matches the upper-right corner. Make the LOWER CORNER layer active and diminish the layer's opacity until it balances the UPPER CORNER layer; in this case 78% should do it (**Figure 3.15i**).

Here is the result (**Figure 3.15j**).

NOTE: I didn't correct this balance problem when I was merging the four images into one, because it didn't manifest itself until I did the white- and black-point compensations. That's often the way things go. To develop a dynamic approach to workflow, give yourself permission to adapt and be flexible.

Figure 3.15J

Directing the unconscious eye

Every act of creation has to start first with an act of destruction.

—Pablo Picasso

In the previous chapter, I defined the human eye as an organic optical device. But this *eye* is by no means conscious. True, the eye evolved from migrated brain tissue, but it does not think. It sees what it sees and does so in a very specific manner.

But I believe that humans are in possession of another "eye," the conscious one; one that gives meaning to what we see. The conscious eye cannot see the how of what is recorded, just as the unconscious eye cannot see the why of what is seen. To this point, you have made decisions on how to manipulate an image so it will speak to the conscious eye of the viewer. You have done that by causing the unconscious eye to go where you wanted it to go, so that the story would be seen the way you determined it should. That was done by using the alphabet of the photograph. The alphabet of the

photograph is found in understanding that the organic optical device first recognizes light areas and then moves to dark ones, sees high-contrast before low-contrast areas, records areas of high sharpness before low sharpness, notices areas in focus before those that are blurred, and focuses on highly color-saturated areas before moving to less-saturated ones. From this alphabet, we build words and sentences, and from words and sentences come the expression and language of the photograph. By controlling the way the unconscious eye sees is another facet of control by which we cause shape to become the unwitting ally of color.

Previously you created a pattern interrupted to control the unconscious eye. Now you will do that by working from dark-to-light (not from light-to-dark) to remove the light that does not belong in this bright, but slightly flat, image.

Step 3: Varying Lightness and Darkness with Blending Modes

In Chapters One and Two, you learned that when you darken an image, you also increase its color saturation. This was why you used the Luminosity blending mode for darkening, because it affects only the light-to-dark aspect of the color. In this next step, you are going to selectively vary both lightness and darkness in this image by using the blending modes Multiply and Screen. The Multiply blending mode doubles the density of the image, and the Screen blending mode halves it. Normally, when you increase the image's density, it gets darker and its color saturation increases. Conversely, when you decrease the image's density, you reduce the color saturation. These are important considerations, because you control the path followed by the unconscious eye through the use not only of light and dark, but also of color saturation.

1. Create an image mapping layer. This will be the first of three image maps you will create for the process of editing the image's light-to-dark/dark-to-light aspect. Name this layer L2D LUM IM for "Light to Dark Luminosity Blending Mode." You are already familiar with working from light-to-dark, so it's a good place to start.

2. Select the Pencil tool and choose magenta as the foreground color. Write in the percentages by which the image needs to be changed. I chose 0% for the left flower, 25% for the right flower, and 50% for the back flower (**Figure 3.16a**).

Analyze the image and decide where you want the unconscious eye to go. I wanted the viewer's eye to go to the left flower, then the right flower, and then to the back one. You will do this by *adding* darkness to *remove* lightness. When using the Luminosity blending mode, you will be dealing only with the light-to-dark aspect of the image, not its actual color.

NOTE: The percentages shown may not reflect the absolute amounts of opacity required to create the effect you want, but their ratios always reflect their relationships.

FIGURE 3.16A *The first of several light-to-dark image maps.*

3. Create another image map and name it D 2 L MULTI IM. This will be the image map for the dark-to-light work you are going to do with the Multiply blending mode (**Figure 3.16b**).

NOTE: Because the eye tracks from high-to-low color saturation I decided to reinforce the blues and purples over the greens and yellows. Therefore, in this instance, it's beneficial to increase the saturation when you darken the image.

You are going to use the Multiply blending mode because it doubles the density of the image, which means you will be adding darkness in the form of density. You will also be increasing the saturation of the colors. I did not want to "add" any darkness to the main flowers, but I wanted to add 50% darkness around them and 20% darkness from the top to the middle, as shown in Figure 3.16b.

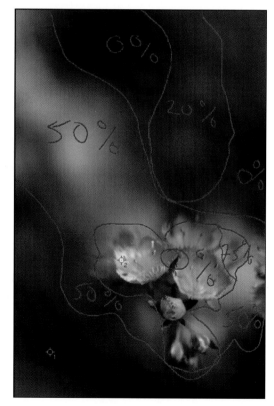

FIGURE 3.16B *The second light-to-dark image map.*

FIGURE 3.17A *The image before applying the Multiply blending mode.*

FIGURE 3.17B *The effect of the Multiply mode.*

FIGURE 3.17C

FIGURE 3.17D

Step 4: Multiply Blending Mode

Hide the image map layer for a moment and look at what happens when you create an adjustment layer and then select the Multiply blending mode.

1. Create a Curves adjustment layer and click OK. Nothing happened, right? Now go to the Layers palette and choose Multiply from the Blending Mode menu.

Here is the image before using Multiply blending mode (**Figure 3.17a**). Using the Multiply blending mode doubled the density of the image (**Figure 3.17b**). It also affected its color saturation, which is desirable here because you want to create the impression that the shadows you saw were actually as deep as they will appear in the final image.

2. Name the Curves adjustment layer L 2 D MULTI CURVES.

3. Fill the layer mask with black. At 50% opacity, select a soft brush about the size of the blurry spot above the flowers (**Figure 3.17c**).

NOTE: If you feel that you need a safety net, you can turn on the image map and brush within the lines.

4. Using white, paint in the blue blurred area behind the flowers, the buds beneath the flowers, and the flowers at the right edge (**Figure. 3.17d**).

FIGURE 3.17E

FIGURE 3.17F

FIGURE 3.17G

FIGURE 3.17H

FIGURE 3.18A

FIGURE 3.18B

5. Reduce the brush to the size of the flower on which you intend to work. Paint over the rearmost flower of the three main ones. It now looks like this (**Figure 3.17e**).

6. Reduce the brush opacity to 20% and click once on the unopened flower (**Figure 3.17f**).

7. Reduce the brush opacity to 10% and click once on the flower to the right and above (**Figures 3.17g** and **3.17h**).

The last thing to do on this layer is to tone down the area just above the blurred blue area on which you first worked. You'll do that because the viewer's eye is drawn to the light area first, instead of to the flowers in the lower part of the image (**Figures 3.18a** and **3.18b**).

The area worked on appears like this on the Curves adjustment layer (**Figure 3.18c**).

The deepening of color and depth of exposure are on track, which is why I had you choose the blending mode Multiply, but some areas have become a little too saturated. You'll revisit them later.

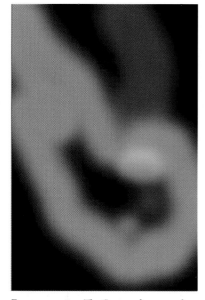

FIGURE 3.18C *The Curves adjustment layer.*

FIGURE 3.19A

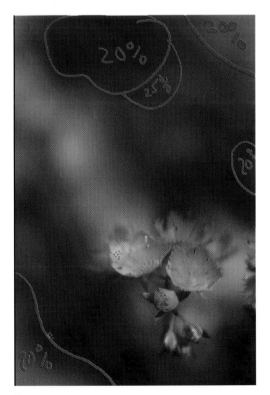

FIGURE 3.19B

Step 5: Dynamic Curves Layer Using the Luminosity Blending Mode

Create another Curves adjustment layer, but rather than a null curve like you just used with Multiply, make it a dynamic one. Adjust the curve and assign it a blending mode, in this case Luminosity, so as to not darken the color by changing its saturation. Do not do this casually. Work on the adjustment layer in a focused way, building its levels by brushing and rebrushing areas to create varying levels of intensity until the image is exactly as you will want to see it in the finished print.

1. Add a Curves layer, and while the Curves dialog is open, drag the center of the curve. (The Input and Output fields should read 147 and 108 respectively.) Fill the layer mask with black. Change the layer's blending mode to Luminosity. Name the layer L2D LUM.

2. With a 20% opacity brush, paint over the areas you mapped in the L2D LUM IM image map. But be subtle; remember, use Photoshop as an emery board, not a jackhammer. The result should look like this (**Figure 3.19a**).

Step 6: Screen Blending Mode

In this last light-to-dark adjustment you are going to use the Screen blending mode. In the last two Curves adjustment layers, you created the overall relationship of light-to-dark and dark-to-light. (As we have seen in this image, sometimes both need to be addressed as if they are separate thoughts.) But there is still work to do. Because the Screen blending mode halves the density of the image, the image will be lightened as well as the color density decreased. What you are doing here is using a little digital fine-grain sandpaper to smooth out some rough spots (**Figure 3.19b**).

FIGURE 3.19C *Screen layer mask.*

FIGURE 3.19D *After.*

1. Create a null Curves adjustment layer (one where you don't adjust the curve itself; instead, just assign it a blending mode) but select Screen mode instead of Multiply. Name this layer L2D SCREEN.

2. Fill the layer mask with black. Select a 20% opacity brush the size of the blurry circular area. Open the blocked-up areas of the lower-left corner, the upper-middle section, and midway down the right side of the image (**Figures 3.19c** and **3.19d**).

NOTE: Whether you start with the Multiply or with the Screen blending mode depends on what the individual image needs. Here, it was probably smart to start with Multiply, since you have been using the depth of the green to reinforce the lightness of the blues and purples.

If you are pleased with the overall color density, it's time to enhance the image's three-dimensionality by working on its range of light-to-dark. It's also time to begin the next phase; defining relationships of contrast, sharpness, and saturation, so that they fit the original vision of the finished image.

The Dance of Sharpness, Saturation, and Contrast

Step 1: Adjust Saturation

You are going to do your first-level saturation adjustment in this image, not in the LAB space, as you did in Chapter 2, but here in the RGB color space. The reason for doing it this way, in this image, is that you need to make fairly small changes, and you can't be sure how much color boost you're going to need or want, if any, until after you're done addressing the issues of blue color cast, contrast, and sharpness.

1. Create a Hue/Saturation adjustment layer. Bring the saturation to 100% so you can analyze the color (**Figure 3.20a**). There is a lot of yellow in the green; the purples are more blue than cyan; there is magenta only in the highlights; and the flowers are more yellowish-green than one would have thought. Lower the saturation to 0 and move the Hue/Saturation dialog off the image.

2. Choose Blues from the Edit menu (Cmd-5/Ctrl-5). I start with the blues because the Hue/ Saturation layer revealed that there was more blue than cyan in the image. Raise the saturation until the image begins to posterize (at about 68), then lower it until it looks appealing to the eye (about 35). Increase the lightness to about 21, which will improve the quality of the saturation of the image's blues (**Figure 3.20b**).

NOTE: Keyboard shortcuts for all of the colors are located to the right on the Edit menu.

NOTE: You may wonder why I chose to increase the lightness here. Why not just leave it alone or darken it, since darkening increases saturation? The problem is that when you darken a color, you also flatten or deaden it. So unless that's the effect you want, consider boosting lightness.

FIGURE 3.20C

FIGURE 3.20D

FIGURE 3.20E

FIGURE 3.20F *The Hue/ Saturation layer mask after painting over the greens.*

3. Repeat the process with the cyans. Posterization appears at saturation 83, so back it down to 21. That gives the image a bump, but without any posterization. Boost the lightness to 41 (**Figures 3.20c** and **3.20d**).

4. Select Master from the Edit menu, boost the global saturation to 20%, and click OK. This creates a problem; the green areas are too saturated, and slight posterization is occurring (**Figure 3.20e**). Select the Brush tool. At 100% opacity, paint over the green areas with black paint to hide them (**Figure 3.20f**).

The image should now look like this (**Figure 3.20g**).

5. Do "The Move" and name the new layer MASTER 3.

FIGURE 3.20G

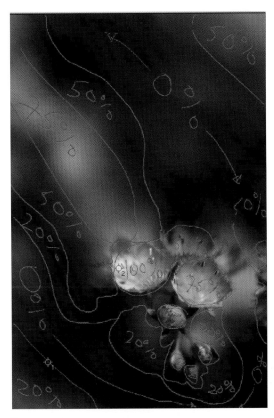

FIGURE 3.21A

FIGURE 3.21B

Step 2: Remove the Blue Sunlight Cast
Using the Nik Skylight Filter

NOTE: You are going to create an image map after the fact instead of before, because you won't know what you want to remove until you actually run the filter.

1. Duplicate the MASTER 3 layer. Name the layer you just created SKYLIGHT. Choose Filter > Nik Color Efex Pro 2.0: traditional filters > Skylight filter. Click OK to run the filter using the default settings.

2. Create a new layer and name it SKYLIGHT IM.

3. Select the Pencil tool, and pick a new color with which to write as you map out the next steps. (I chose a light blue.) The changes on the image map will guide the viewer's eye through the image, from light to dark, starting with the cluster of flowers in the lower-right corner. The eye should then go first to the upper-left flower, the middle-right flower, and finally to the lower-right flower.

4. So as not to affect the green areas, mark them 0%. Next do the edges, and lastly the background areas. The resulting image map looks like this (**Figure 3.21a**).

5. Make the SKYLIGHT layer active. Create a layer mask filled with black, and brush in with white using the varying levels of opacity mapped out in the SKYLIGHT IM image map (**Figure 3.21b**).

6. Do "The Move," name the layer CONTRAST, then duplicate the layer and name the duplicated layer SHARPEN. Turn off the SHARPEN layer, make the CONTRAST layer active, and save the file.

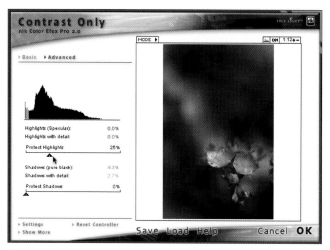

FIGURE 3.22A

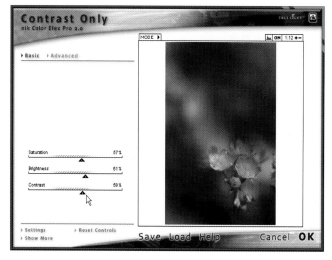

FIGURE 3.22B

Step 3: Selective Contrast

Using the Nik Contrast Only filter

1. Choose Filter > Nik Color Efex Pro 2.0: traditional filters and select the Contrast Only filter. In the Contrast Only dialog, click Advanced (**Figure 3.22a**).

2. Start by adjusting the contrast. Move the Contrast slider to the right until the image starts to seriously posterize and the shadows block up.

Here, this happens at the right edge of the yellow zone on the Contrast slider, or 66%. This is obviously too much, but it's usually easier soften an effect than to boost it. When using layer masks, it's also better to be a little over than a little under. You can always lower the opacity of the effect, either by using the Fade command on the Edit menu or by lowering the opacity of the layer after you have created the relationship you like.

3. Back the slider down until you hit the fine edge between posterizing and not posterizing. For this image, that's 58%. Now adjust the brightness. First make the image too bright, at 75%, and then adjust it down to 61%. Lastly, adjust the saturation. Bring it up to 64%, then back it down to 57% (**Figure 3.22b**).

4. Go to Advanced. You want to protect the image's highlights, so you need to tell the filter where to stop boosting contrast. For this image, set the cutoff at 25% for the highlights and leave it at the default setting (0%) for the shadows. Click OK to apply the filter.

5. Create a new image map layer, name it CONTRAST IM, and move it above MASTER 4 COPY 3.

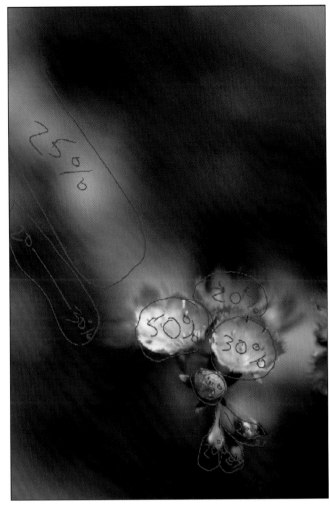

FIGURE 3.23 *The image map of contrast areas.*

6. You will now map the areas where you want the effect of contrast to show through, and where you don't. You want to emphasize the flowers in the foreground, so mark the left flower 50%, the rear flower 20%, and the lower right flower 30%. Mark the smaller flowers (beneath the main ones) 20%. You also want to impart some character to the bright area in the background, so mark that 25% (**Figure 3.23**).

7. Create a layer mask filled with black. (If you are using the classic contrast Curves approach, fill the adjustment layer's layer mask with black.) Do the appropriate brushwork.

Without the Nik contrast filter

This is the classic way to create a contrast curve, and it is much better than using Photoshop's Brightness/Contrast adjustment.

1. Duplicate the layer MASTER 4 three times. Turn off the eyeballs of layers MASTER 4 COPY 3, and MASTER 4 COPY 2. Make the layer MASTER 4 COPY active and rename it CONTRAST.

2. Create a Curves adjustment layer. Click the center point of the curve to lock it. Place the mouse pointer over the curve, two grid lines up and right. Drag that point up and to the left to increase the contrast to a level that is visually pleasing. Don't drag too far; you just need a small amount. Click OK. Name the layer CONTRAST.

3. Create a layer mask filled with black, and do the appropriate brushwork.

FIGURE 3.24A

Step 4: Selective Sharpening by Color

To analyze the image, make the MASTER 4 COPY 3 the active layer, then create a new layer and name it SHARPEN FLOWERS IM.

Select the Pencil tool and pick a new color with which to write. (I chose cyan.) Zoom into the area of the flowers (**Figure 3.24a**). You are going to map out where you want the eye to go. Do this even if you aren't going to be sharpening using the Nik Sharpener Pro 2.0 filter. Regardless of the sharpening method you use, you still should map out a sharpening strategy.

To my eye, it's apparent that the core of this image consists of circles that interrupt a pattern of diagonals. You'll play up that spiral effect, starting with the pistils of the flowers (**Figures 3.24b**, **3.24c**, and **3.24d**).

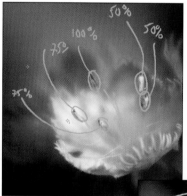

FIGURE 3.24C

FIGURE 3.24B

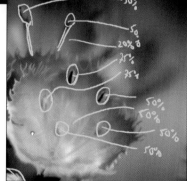

FIGURE 3.24D

FIGURE 3.24E

FIGURE 3.24F

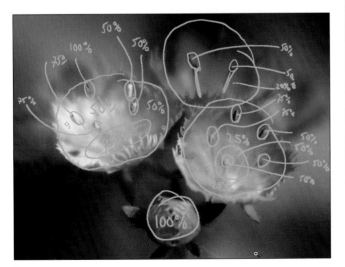

FIGURE 3.24G

1. Use 100% for the lower flower because it's a bit too out of focus, and it needs all the help it can get (**Figure 3.24e**).

2. Now, define the secondary areas of sharpness in order to get the viewer's eye to move around the flower the way you want it to (**Figures 3.24f** and **3.24g**). When you've finished, hide the image map layer.

3. Create a new layer, name it LEAVES SHARPEN IM, and repeat the process, this time paying attention to the leaves that surround the flowers (**Figure 3.24h**). When you've finished, hide the image map layer.

Using the Nik Sharpener Pro 2.0 filter

If you have the Nik Sharpener Pro 2.0 filter, continue with this section. If you don't, skip to the next section.

1. Duplicate the SHARPEN layer. Turn off the eyeball of the layer you just duplicated, make SHARPEN the active layer, and rename it FLOWERS SHARPEN. Zoom in on the flowers and turn the eyeball on for the image map SHARPEN FLOWERS IM.

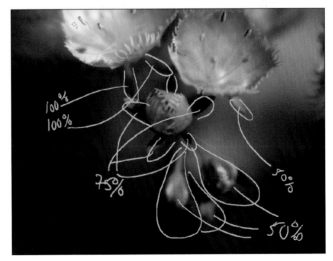

FIGURE 3.24H

2. Choose the appropriate printer output. In my case, that is Filter > Nik Sharpener Pro 2.0 > Inkjet: Epson (**Figure 3.24i**). Leave the viewing distance set to Auto and the paper dimensions to what comes up in the dialog.

3. Use the Paper Type slider to select the kind of paper on which you will ultimately print and then the Printer resolution you plan to use. (Because I was creating a fine-art print, I moved the slider to Texture & Fine Art and chose Somerset Velvet. The printer resolution for this paper is 2880 × 1440.)

4. Switch to the Advanced pane of the dialog.

5. Click the bottom eyedropper, sample one of the green leaves in the dialog, and move the slider to 0%. In this sharpening layer, you want to sharpen only the blues and purples, not the greens (**Figure 3.24j**).

6. With the eyedropper that is the second from the bottom, select the leaves of the lower bottom buds (where the green is more yellow) and move the slider for that color to 0%.

7. Click the third eyedropper from the bottom, sample the lower front flower, and leave the slider at 100%.

8. Click on the second eyedropper from the top, sample the light purple in the inside of the top left flower, and leave the slider at 100% (**Figure 3.24k**).

9. With the top eyedropper, select the lightest purple in the main flower.

10. Add a layer mask filled with black, and hide the layer for the moment.

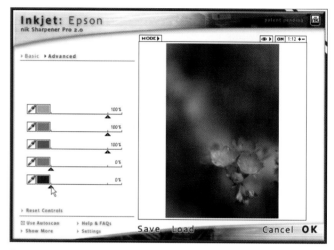

Figure 3.24j

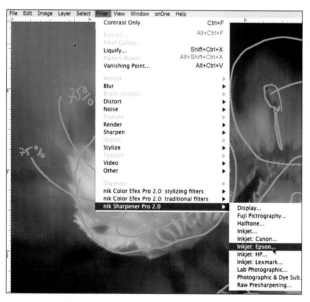

Figure 3.24i

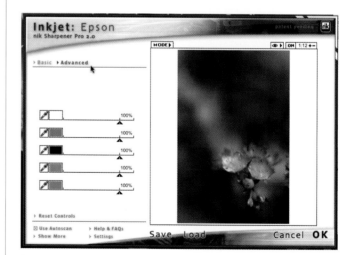

Figure 3.24k

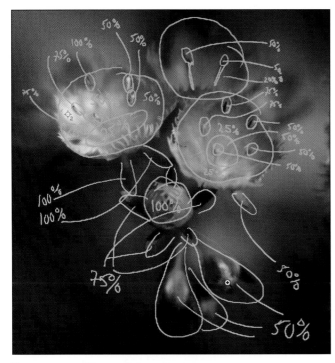

FIGURE 3.24L *The overall sharpening image map.*

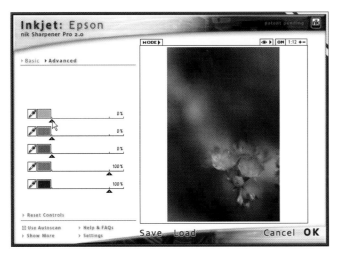

FIGURE 3.24M

11. Turn on the eyeball for the layer SHARPEN COPY and make that layer the active one. Rename it LEAVES SHARPEN. If you are using image maps, turn on the image map for the leaves (**Figure 3.24l**).

12. Launch the Sharpener Pro 2.0 > Inkjet: Epson filter. Switch to the Advanced pane; reverse the sharpening by moving the green sliders to 100%, and the blue-purple and white sliders to 0% (**Figure 3.24m**).

When you've finished, continue with the "Final sharpening steps" section, below.

Using Photoshop's Unsharp Mask filter

If you don't have the Nik Sharpener Pro 2.0 filter, you can use Photoshop's Unsharp Mask Filter. (See "Using Photoshop's Unsharp Mask filter" in Chapter 2.)

When you've finished, continue with "Final Sharpening Steps," below.

Final Sharpening Steps

If you worked through the Nik Sharpener Pro procedure, make sure the layer FLOWERS SHARPEN is active.

If you used the Unsharp Mask method, activate the layer SHARPEN.

1. Create a black-filled layer mask. Zoom in on the upper-left flower. With a 50% opacity brush that is about the size of the pistils, brush and rebrush the pistils for all the flowers, increasing their sharpness (**Figure 3.25a**).

FIGURE 3.25A *Sharpening a pistil.*

2. Increase the brush to the size of the lower flower and brush that flower at 100% opacity (**Figures 3.25b** and **3.25c**).

3. Paint on the inner parts of the flowers using the opacities you marked on the FLOWERS SHARPEN image map. The result can be seen on the FLOWERS SHARPEN layer mask (**Figure 3.25d**).

4. Hide the FLOWERS SHARPEN layer and make LEAVES SHARPEN visible and active. (If you used the Unsharp Mask filter, keep working on the SHARPEN layer.) Also, make the LEAVES SHARPEN IM image map visible.

5. Repeat the process of painting with white on the layer mask using the opacities that you sketched in earlier. Here are the changes in the lower flower area (**Figures 3.25e**, **3.25f**, **3.25g**, and **3.25h**).

6. Make the layer FLOWERS SHARPEN (or SHARPEN if you used the Unsharp Mask filter) active, and turn off any image maps. Do "The Move," rename the new layer MASTER 4, and save the file.

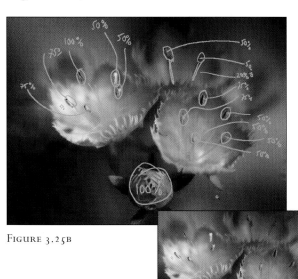

FIGURE 3.25B

FIGURE 3.25E

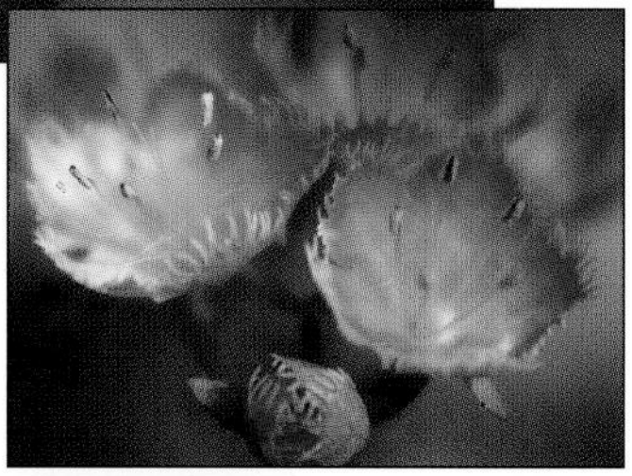

FIGURE 3.25C

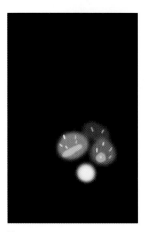

FIGURE 3.25D

FIGURE 3.25F

FIGURE 3.25G

FIGURE 3.25H *Sharpening the lower flower area.*

Selective Neutral Density Using Lighting Effects

If you are working in Photoshop CS or CS2, you have gone as far as you can go working in 16-bit color. As noted before, digital image artifacting is cumulative, and every time you do something in Photoshop, you are dumping data and creating artifacts that you don't want seen in your final print. So you'll convert the image from 16-bit to 8-bit. You will then exploit a little-known side of Photoshop's Render > Lighting Effects filter. You are going to use the Lighting Effects filter in a way that the engineers at Adobe may not have intended: not to light the image, but to de-light it.

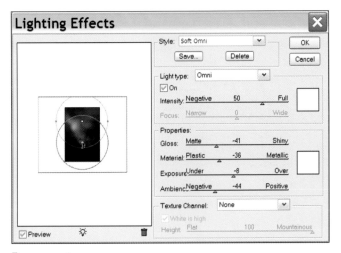

FIGURE 3.26A

Step 1: De-Lighting with the Lighting Effects Filter

1. Select "Save As" From the file pull-down menu. Name the new file BLUE MASTER FLOWER LIGHTING 8BIT.psd. Turn off the layers in the Save As option box. Close the file BLUE MASTER FLOWER 16BIT.psd and open the file BLUE MASTER FLOWER LIGHTING 8BIT.psd. Convert the image from 16-bit color to 8-bit color (Image > Mode > 8 Bits/Channel). Duplicate the background layer, rename it LIGHTING ND (for neutral density), and save the file.

2. Choose Filter > Render > Lighting Effects. As a style, select Soft Omni. Click the center point and drag it to the middle of the upper-left flower (**Figure 3.26a**).

3. Click the lower anchor point of the circle, and drag it until the circle is about the same size as the upper-left flower (**Figure 3.26b**).

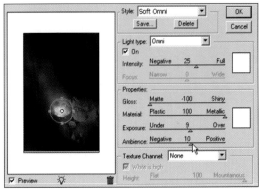

FIGURE 3.26B

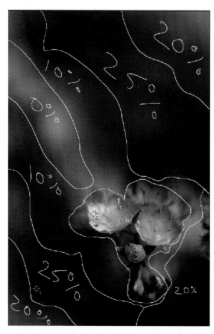

Figure 3.27a

Figure 3.27b

4. In the Properties area of the Lighting Effects dialog, move the Gloss slider all the way to Matte (–100) and the Material slider to Metallic (+100). Increase Ambience from the default of –44 to a point where you can see the background, which for this image is 10.

5. Under Light Type, lower Intensity until the flower is no longer blown out. For this image, the percentage is 25.

6. Under Properties, increase the exposure from the default of –8 to where the left flower is again lit; for this image that's 9. Click OK.

Step 2: Marking the Lighting Image Map

In black-and-white silver photography, printers sometimes slightly darken the edges of a print to draw the viewer's eye to the center of the picture. To apply that technique here, give the outer edges a value of 20%. This also makes the image appear more three-dimensional.

1. Create a new image map layer named LIGHTING ND IM, select the Pencil tool, and write with a new color. (I chose yellow.)

2. To deepen the greens, outline those areas on the image map and assign them a value of 25%. To slightly darken the periphery of the blue-purple area behind the main flowers, assign them a value of 10%. Leave the top ridge alone and give it a value of 0% (**Figure 3.27a**).

3. Now, move on to the flowers. You added some light to this image when you put the Soft Omni light on the upper-front flower, so let's use it. Give this area a value of 50%. In the process, you darkened all the areas around the front flower, so give the back flower a value of 50% as well. The difference here is that you will be darkening, not lightening as you did with the front left flower.

4. Leave the lower left flower alone, and consider the buds. To concentrate on the play of real light and shadows and promote the three-dimensional appearance, assign the buds a value of 50% (**Figure 3.27b**).

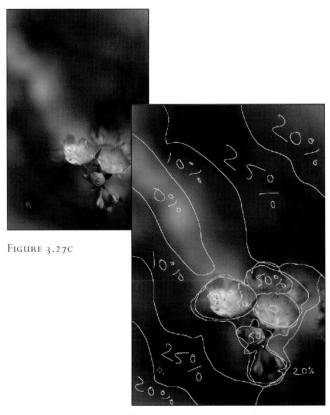

FIGURE 3.27C

FIGURE 3.27D

FIGURE 3.27E

5. Make LIGHTING ND active again, add a black-filled mask, and do the brushwork (**Figures 3.27c**, **3.27d**, and **3.27e**).

Here is what appears on the layer mask (**Figure 3.27f**).

6. What you have done is a little too dark (**Figure 3.27g**), so reduce the opacity of the layer to 51%. Select the Screen blending mode. (Remember that the Screen blending mode halves the density of the image, whereas the Multiply blending mode doubles the density.)

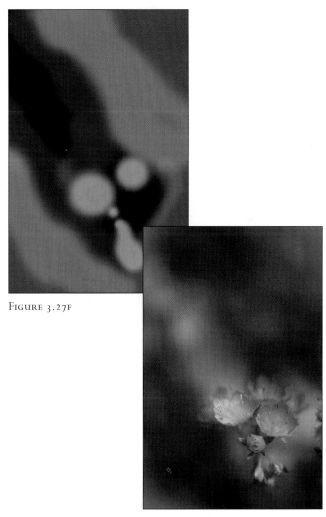

FIGURE 3.27F

FIGURE 3.27G

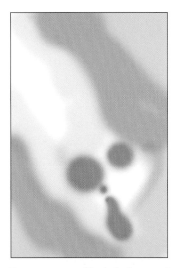

FIGURE 3.27H *Here's the layer mask.*

FIGURE 3.27I *Here's the image.*

Step 3: Increasing Saturation in the LAB color space

1. Save the file. Next, "Save As" in the File Save Option dialog box and click the layers off. Name the file BLUE MASTER FLOWER LIGHTING LAB 8BIT.psd.

2. Now open the file BLUE MASTER FLOWER LIGHTING LAB 8BIT.psd. Go to Image >Mode and select LAB. You have just converted the file to the LAB color space.

3. Create a Curves adjustment layer. (Be sure to Alt-/Option-click on the grid to get the small grid.) Select "a." Move the top and bottom anchor points over one grid line.

4. Now Select "b." Move the top anchor point over one grid line and the bottom over one grid line. Make a Master layer (do "The Move"). Save the file.

5. Shift-drag the Master layer onto the BLUE MASTER FLOWER LIGHTING 8BIT.psd file. Name this layer LAB.

6. Ctrl-click on the layer mask of the LIGHTING layer. Go to Select > Inverse (Shft-Ctrl-I/Shft-Cmd-I) and create a layer mask on the LAB layer. The color is still a little too "deep," so lower the layer's opacity. For this image it's 75%.

7. Make a Master layer (do "The Move"). Save the file.

If you make a print and find that areas of high blur exhibit a stepping pattern that looks like a topographical map, you are seeing banding posterization. According to Peter Bauer, this "occurs when similar values are forced to a single value, creating artificially large differences between adjoining steps." Banding posterization has a tendency to occur in the very blurry areas of an image, because the computer is trying to linearize the randomness of the blur. There are several ways to address this issue, but the quickest way is to add noise to the affected areas. The noise breaks up the banding. Generally, you want to use Monochromatic Gaussian noise. To do this, start by Alt-/Opt-clicking on the Create New Layer icon of the Layers palette. This will bring up the New Layer dialog box. In the Name box type NOISE; from the Mode pull-down, select the blending mode Soft Light; and check the Fill with Soft-Light neutral color (50% gray). Click OK. Go to Filter > Noise > Add Noise. In the dialog box, select Gaussian Noise and check Monochromatic. The size of the image file determines how much noise to add. I have found that the range is between 2 and 8. As a rule, it's better to add as little noise as possible. The rule of thumb is, the smaller the file, the less noise. The bigger the file, the more noise.

Children Play, They Don't Take Notes. Adults Take Notes …

If you've made it through this long chapter, hopefully, you're convinced of the power and subtlety of image harvesting. You have also had a master class in directing the viewer's unconscious eye.

I believe that once you understand how to control color, you will have complete mastery of the images that you create. I also believe that you have to learn the rules before you can effectively break them. But if you make all of this a game, the playfulness and spontaneity that you bring to the process will be inherent in the image. It is from this sort of spontaneity that the truth of your experience is captured.

In the next chapter, we'll tackle two related but very different concepts: lighting and drama.

Figure 4.1

Figure 4.2 *The* Stardust *image*.

Chapter 4

Classic Studio Lighting

What's the best type of light? Why that would be available light…
and by available light I mean any damn light that is available.

—W. Eugene Smith

In this chapter, we will use Photoshop to emulate the look of a classic Hollywood glamour photograph, working with an image that I've entitled *Stardust*. In the following chapter, I'll explain how to convert *Stardust* into a continuous-tone, black-and-white image.

Creating *Stardust*

When most people think of movie-star images from the 1930s and '40s, George Hurrell's classic photographs come to mind. With his iconic portraits of Greta Garbo, Jean Harlow, and Gary Cooper, Hurrell invented the Hollywood glamour photograph, and his dramatic use of light was second to none.

Hurrell most often used two focusable light sources, which he diffused and placed above and on either side of his subject. This type of lighting became known as "butterfly lighting" because of the hallmark shadow it produced under the subject's nose.

He lit his famous subjects with movie or hot lights, not strobes, and photographed them with an 8 × 10 view camera, not an SLR. He didn't have the luxury of roll film or Compact-Flash cards. He would engage his actor subjects in dialogue, and from time to time he'd click the shutter. The images he captured were the result of those experiences.

NOTE: An early version of this chapter appeared in *The PhotoshopWorld Dream Team Book*, Vol. 1 (New Riders/Peachpit Press, 2005).

In *Stardust*, the model on the bearskin was lit naturally with reflected sunlight. This takes advantage of the unique characteristic of sunlight to be both directional and ambient at the same time. The technique selected to light the base capture image is called "board-to-board reflecting." It's used to get light from someplace other than a point light source (in this case the sun), or to make the light source appear to be farther from the subject than it actually is. (See sidebar.) Here, that technique was the best way to evenly light the subject with the best type of light—reflected sunlight.

NOTE: The reason I prefer to use reflected natural light is that it has a glowing quality that I have not seen in any other type of light. Also, when doing environmental portraiture, this approach gives me light that is simultaneously directional and ambient: directional because the reflector provides a point light source; ambient because the light is naturally present. This allows the subject more freedom of movement, which typically produces a more spontaneous photograph. I have found that the poses people naturally assume are often far more interesting than those I suggest.

I chose this lighting technique, not only for aesthetic reasons, but to save time and money. All I needed were two light stands with light disk holders, and two reflectors. Setup and breakdown times were insignificant, and the reflected sunlight was a bonus; again, the more you know about the middle, the more informed your choices can be at the beginning (**Figure 4.3**).

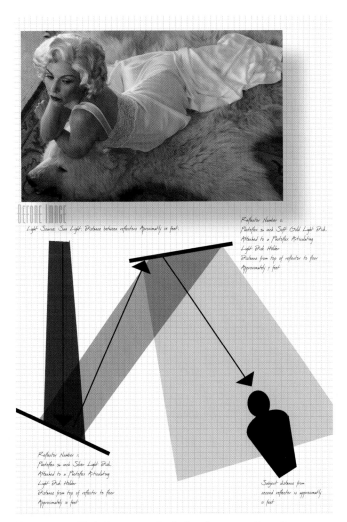

Light Source: Sun Light. Distance between reflectors Approximately 10 feet.

Reflector Number 2:
Photoflex 36 inch Soft Gold Light Disk.
Attached to a Photoflex Articulating
Light Disk Holder
Distance from top of reflector to floor
Approximately 7 feet

Reflector Number 1:
Photoflex 36 inch Silver Light Disk.
Attached to a Photoflex Articulating
Light Disk Holder
Distance from top of reflector to floor
Approximately 10 feet

Subject distance from
second reflector is approximately
10 feet

FIGURE 4.3 *The lighting setup for the* Stardust *image: Two reflectors direct sunlight onto the subject.*

Casting Light on the Stardust Model

The lighting technique used in creating this image is often referred to as board-to-board reflecting. The model was lit by bouncing sunlight off two 36-inch reflectors. The first one, a Photoflex Silver reflector, directed light onto the second reflector, which reflected light onto the subject. The combination created a slightly warm light.

This type of light is referred to as "long light"—the kind that occurs in the Northern Hemisphere during late afternoons in February and October, when the sun is close to the horizon. Because the light comes through the thickest part of the atmosphere, it travels farther and scatters more blue light, letting the longer-wave-length (warmer) colors shine through. This type of light produces long shadows and generally warm tones.

Reflector #1: Photoflex 36-inch Silver LiteDisc attached to a Photoflex Articulating LiteDisc Holder. Distance from top of reflector to floor, approximately 10 feet. Silver increases the specular highlights and yields a high-contrast image. (This reflector was angled slightly upward and was the lower of the two.)

Reflector #2: Photoflex 36-inch Soft Gold LiteDisc attached to a Photoflex Articulating LiteDisc Holder. Distance from top of reflector to floor, approximately 7 feet. Soft Gold combines gold and silver in a zigzag pattern, giving a warm tone to the light it reflects. (This reflector was angled slightly downward, onto the subject and was the higher of the two.)

Measure Twice, Cut Once

Step 1: Analyzing the Image and Creating Image Maps

As you have seen, it's easy to be overwhelmed by the amount of work to be done on any image, whether simple or complex. In order to avoid that feeling, it's best to break the task into manageable steps and attack them one at a time. The first step is to map out the image. Next, define the issues you must resolve in the image and how you want to approach them. Always work from global to granular. For me, the issues in the *Stardust* image are:

- Remove the CCD color cast.
- Remove the blue color cast from sunlight.
- Create areas of selective depth of field.
- Retouch the face (see note, below).
- Light the image.

With those five issues in mind, I will show you how to create image maps and begin to develop a workflow specific to this image.

NOTE: For the *Stardust* image, I did some retouching work on the woman's face that entailed adding several more layers to the ones I describe in this chapter. I will skip those steps here, in order to focus on creating the glamour lighting effect. However, they are included in the 100ppi reference version of the file that you will find on the DVD.

Step 2: Removing CCD Color Cast

1. Using the Threshold adjustment layer method, as described in previous chapters, identify the black and white points. You are looking for "meaningful" black for the black point. For the white point, choose a point as close to the first white pixel as you can get, whether or not you can recognize shape or structure within it.

Once the white and black points are established, mark them with color samplers. The white and black color samplers are visible in this image as crosshair targets #1 and #2 (**Figures 4.4a, 4.4b,** and **4.4c**).

FIGURE 4.4A *Color sampler marking the black point.*

FIGURE 4.4B *Color sampler marking the white point.*

FIGURE 4.4C *The image after the initial color cast has been removed.*

FIGURE 4.5 *After applying the Nik Skylight filter.*

FIGURE 4.6A *The image map of how you are going to create selective depth of field.*

2. Do "The Move" (Ctrl-Alt-Shift-E/Cmd-Option-Shift-E. For CS and below, press Ctrl-Alt-Shift/Cmd-Option-Shift, then type N and then E), and name the layer SKYLIGHT.

3. Select Skylight Filter from the Nik Color Efex Pro 2.0: traditional filters menu. For this image, leave the default setting of 25% and click OK to run the filter (**Figure 4.5**).

4. Do a Save As, save the file as a Photoshop document (.psd), and name it STARDUST 16BIT.

Step 3: Creating Selective Depth of Field to Replicate Optical Lens Blur

Because we are trying to create a probable believability, we have to make sure that all of our choices mimic reality as captured with a glass lens. When you use such a lens, the effects are optically, and not digitally, created. One of these effects is that as blur increases, there is a tendency for contrast to diminish. This does not occur in Photoshop when blurring the image with Gaussian Blur or using just the Lens Blur tool. This step will illustrate how to realistically replicate optical lens blur.

With this consideration in mind, you will be working with two aspects of controlling the unconscious eye: in focus to blur, and high contrast to low contrast. That's because you want the eye to move from the face down the body. Specifically, you want the model's face to be the central point of focus, then the front part of the model's body, then the bear's face, and then the upper background, which is the most out of focus. So blur and contrast go hand in hand for this image. Sharpness will be used very selectively (**Figure 4.6a**).

1. Duplicate the SKYLIGHT layer and name the new layer BLUR. Duplicate the BLUR layer and name it CONTRAST. Turn off the CONTRAST layer and make the BLUR layer active.

2. Choose Filter > Blur > Gaussian Blur, and use a radius of 8.8 pixels (**Figures 4.6b** and **4.6c**).

NOTE: The amount of blur you apply to an image depends on the size of the file. The bigger the file, the higher the radius number or amount of blur. For this image, you want to blur it to the point where you can still see major image structure detail, but minor detail is smoothed out. For this reason, I chose the model's face as the area to put in the preview box.

FIGURE 4.6B *The Gaussian Blur preview box.*

FIGURE 4.6C *Applying the Gaussian Blur filter to the BLUR layer.*

3. For the BLUR layer, create a layer mask filled with black.

4. Select a brush at an opacity of 75% and paint with white over the background of the upper part of the image. This reveals the blurred effect, which suggests shallow depth of field.

5. Change the opacity to 50% and brush the area from behind the model's knees, all the way to the bear's arm. At an opacity of 25%, paint the area just beneath the head of the bear, back into the area that you just brushed at 50%. Lower the layer opacity to 75 % (**Figures 4.6d** and **4.6e**).

FIGURE 4.6D *The blurring effect is revealed only in certain areas of the image by painting on a layer mask.*

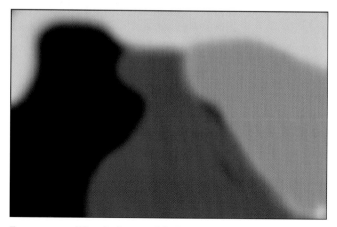

FIGURE 4.6E *What the layer mask looks like.*

FIGURE 4.6F *Selective contrast applied.*

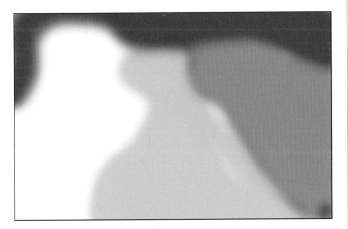

FIGURE 4.6G *The CONTRAST layer mask.*

6. Make the CONTRAST layer the active one. Select the Contrast Only filter from the Nik Color Efex Pro 2.0: traditional filters menu. The settings I came up with for this image were Saturation 52, Brightness 54, and Contrast 62. Click OK.

NOTE: I didn't protect the shadows or highlights because the image didn't need it.

7. Ctrl/Cmd-click on the BLUR layer's layer mask and invert it (Shift-Ctrl-I/Shift-Cmd-I). Create a layer mask on the CONTRAST layer and lower the layer opacity to 75 % (**Figures 4.6f** and **4.6g**).

Step 4: Using Curves to Create Dark-to-Light Areas

Now that you have created the desired depth of field and a more realistic relationship between in-focus-to-blur and contrast, it's time to start building up the image's light-to-dark/dark-to-light relationship. Again, you want the unconscious eye to move from the model's face to the left side of her body, then to the right. Here's the image map of how to do it (**Figure 4.7a**):

FIGURE 4.7A *The dark-to-light image map.*

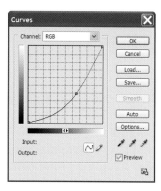

FIGURE 4.7B *Creating a curve to darken all but the bright highlights in the image.*

FIGURE 4.7C *What the image looks like after darkening in the Normal blending mode.*

FIGURE 4.7D *The Luminosity blending mode applies an adjustment to only the brightness values in the image, leaving color values uneffected.*

1. Create a Curves adjustment layer. Click the center of the curve and drag it diagonally toward the lower right-hand corner, making sure not to clip the curve. Click OK to accept the change and close the dialog. Name this layer D2L LUM CURVE. This adjustment substantially darkens the image, except for the extreme highlights (**Figures 4.7b** and **4.7c**).

NOTE: To get a smaller grid pattern, Alt/Option-click on the grid.

2. Change the D2L CURVES adjustment layer's blending mode from Normal to Luminosity. This ensures that the adjustment layer effects only the image's lightness and darkness, not its color (**Figure 4.7d**).

NOTE: Darkening an image generally increases color saturation. Using the Luminosity blending mode applies the adjustment to the gray value (the luminescence) of each pixel, while preserving the color.

3. Following the image map and painting with black, brush in the face at 100%, the arms and front of the hair at 50%, and the back of the dress at 20% (**Figures 4.7e** and **4.7f**).

Remember to increase and decrease your brush size where appropriate. One brush size does not fit all applications. To do that, use the bracket key (located next to the letter P). The left bracket key makes the brush smaller, the right bracket key makes it bigger.

Step 5: Creating Light-to-Dark Areas and Selectively Changing Apparent Contrast

As discussed in Chapter 2, contrast is the difference in brightness between the light and dark areas of a picture. If there is a large difference between the light and dark areas, then the result is an image with high contrast.

In Step 3 of this lesson, we increased and decreased contrast in relationship to depth of field. In Step 4, we addressed creating areas of dark-to-light by adding "darkness" to the image. The unconscious eye tracks from the lightest to the darkest area.

In this next step, you will further reinforce the movement of the unconscious eye from light-to-dark by selectively changing the apparent contrast of the image. (You have already created the relationship you like between light-to-dark and high-to-low-contrast.) How you are going to accomplish this is by creating two Curves adjustment layers: one that will address the image's overall lightness and another that will address the image's overall darkness.

FIGURE 4.7E *The image after selective painting.*

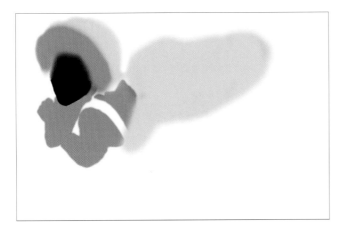

FIGURE 4.7F *The layer mask of the D2L CURVES adjustment layer.*

1. Create a Curves adjustment layer. In the dialog, click the curve's center point and move it toward the upper-left corner, making sure that the arc of the curve is maintained and that it doesn't flatten along the top or left side of the graph. Click OK. Select the blending mode Luminosity and name this layer L2D 1 LUM (**Figures 4.8a** and **4.8b**).

You will use the next Curves adjustment layer a little differently. In order to diminish the apparent contrast between parts of the image, you are going to first darken the image, and then clip the curve.

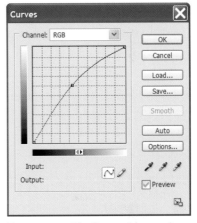

FIGURE 4.8A *The Curves adjustment layer.*

FIGURE 4.8B

2. Create a Curves adjustment layer. In the dialog, click the control point at the upper right end of the curve and drag it downward. Next, add a control point in the middle of the curve and drag it diagonally toward the lower right corner (**Figure 4.8c**). This substantially reduces the entire image's brightness. Click OK to accept the change and close the dialog. Name this layer L2D 2 LUM.

3. With the L2D 2 LUM adjustment layer active, change its blending mode from Normal to Luminosity, and fill the Curves adjustment layer with black. With a brush at 75% opacity, paint the area behind the model. This allows part of the adjustment layer to effect the image. Change the brush opacity to 50%, and paint the area from behind her knees and lower legs to the lower-right corner of the image. With an opacity of 25%, paint the area from behind the bear's ear to the edge of the area you just painted. Finally, lower the brush opacity to 20%, and paint the area just behind the model's back (**Figures 4.9a**, **4.9b**, **4.9c**, and **4.9d**).

FIGURE 4.9A *The contrast image map.*

FIGURE 4.9B *The effect of the L2D 2 LUM curves adjustment layer.*

FIGURE 4.9C *The outcome of the brushwork and what the layer mask looks like. The model's back, lower legs, and the foreground are darkened.*

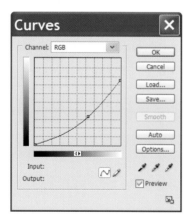

FIGURE 4.8C *Bringing the highlight and midtone point down in a Curves adjustment layer.*

FIGURE 4.9D *The painted areas.*

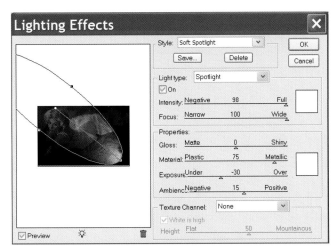

FIGURE 4.10A *The Lighting Effects dialog with the lighting style set to Soft Spotlight.*

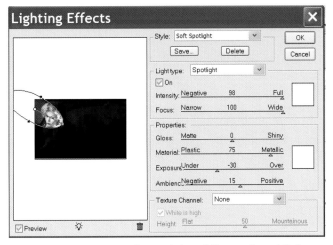

FIGURE 4.10B *Shaping the first spotlight to fall across the model's face.*

Step 6: Placing Lights with the Lighting Effects Filter

You have reached a point where you can no longer work in 16-bit, so the next step is to save the file. In the Save As dialog, uncheck the layers and rename the file STARDUST LIGHTING 8BIT.psd. Next, convert the image from 16-bit to 8-bit.

NOTE: Leave the STARDUST 16BIT.psd file open, so that if you later need something from it, you won't have to waste time re-opening it.

1. From the main menu, choose Image > Mode > 8 Bits/Channel to change the image's color depth.

NOTE: For a discussion of the reasons for converting from 16-bit to 8-bit, see "Lighting the Image with Render > Lighting Effects," in Chapter 1.

2. Create a new layer (Ctrl-J/Cmd-J) and name it LIGHTING BASE LAYER.

3. Choose Filter > Render > Lighting Effects.

4. From the Style pull-down at the top of the Lighting Effects dialog, select Soft Spotlight. Shape this first light by clicking each of the anchor points on the ellipse and dragging them to move the light so that it falls across the model's face (**Figures 4.10a** and **4.10b**).

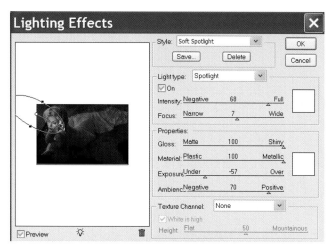

FIGURE 4.10C *Setting exposure, intensity, and focus.*

FIGURE 4.10D *Adding a second light source.*

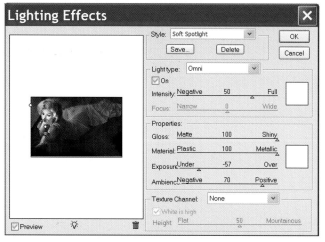

FIGURE 4.10E *Setting the new light source to Omni, adjusting its size, and positioning it over the model's chin.*

5. When the first light is positioned where you want it, go to the Properties section of the dialog and move the Gloss slider to Shiny, the Material slider to Metallic, and increase Ambience until you start to see the rest of the image. Next, move the Exposure slider to –57. In the Light type area of the dialog, adjust the Intensity and Focus sliders to 68 and 7, respectively (**Figure 4.10c**).

6. Add a second light by clicking and dragging the lightbulb icon onto the image preview. For the light type, select Omni. Move the light so that the center point rests right on the model's chin, and decrease the light size by dragging inward on the anchor points (**Figures 4.10d** and **4.10e**).

7. Click the lightbulb icon again, and drag a third light to the area just behind the model's head and above her left thigh. Select Omni as the light type and decrease its intensity to 32 (**Figure 4.11a**).

One other area in this image requires a light adjustment: the bear's eyes.

8. Drag the lightbulb icon to a spot just above the bear's eyes. Drag the anchors so that the light falls across the bear's face. Increase intensity to Full and focus to Wide (**Figures 4.11b** and **4.11c**). Click OK.

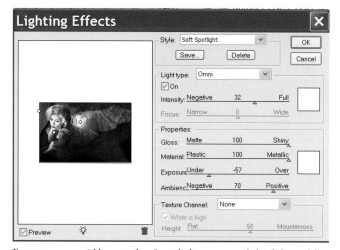

FIGURE 4.11A *Adding another Omni light source just behind the model's head and above her left thigh.*

FIGURE 4.11B *Placing a third light near the bear's face.*

NOTE: This Lighting Effects layer isn't meant to be a finished product, but some aspects of the layer will contribute to the final image.

9. Add a black-filled layer mask to this layer. Select a smaller brush at 25% opacity with white as the foreground color. Paint over the areas across the model's eyes and part of her forehead. Reduce the opacity to 20% and decrease the brush size to a diameter that is slightly smaller than the lips, and drag the brush over them. Still at 20% opacity, paint over the highlighted area along the tops of her thighs and knees. Use 20% opacity for the area around the bear's eyes, then at 50% opacity, paint in the area from the lower leg of the bearskin rug to the upper leg. Don't brush over the area of the model's thighs and knees that you brushed at 20% (**Figures 4.12a**, **4.12b**, and **4.12c**).

FIGURE 4.11C *The result of the Lighting Effects filter on the layer.*

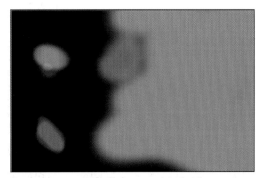

FIGURE 4.12B *What the layer mask looks like.*

FIGURE 4.12A *The Lighting Effects image map.*

FIGURE 4.12C *The result of selectively revealing areas of the layer where the Lighting Effects filter has been applied.*

The objective of this lesson is to believably replicate a very specific approach to lighting—Hurrell's butterfly lighting—as well as replicate the quality of the light that approach produces. You now have an image that is nearly right, but not quite. Even after the corrections you have made that were designed to address the issues of light-to-dark and contrast, you still have some problems in these areas. Because your approach to workflow has been to always give yourself an exit strategy by preserving all the layers that you create, you have built in a way to use the work you have already done, so that you don't have to re-invent the wheel.

10. Make STARDUST 16BIT.psd the active file. (It should still be open.) Make the layer L2D 2 LUM the active layer and shift-drag it onto STARDUST LIGHTING 8BIT.psd. Close the file STARDUST 16BIT.psd. The image should now look like **Figure 4.13**.

11. Make the adjustment layer's layer mask active. With the foreground color set to white, choose a 200-pixel brush at 25% opacity and paint the area around the cheeks and neck, the back and arm, and the arm beneath the face. Reduce the brush to 100 pixels and brush in the area just under the nose. Select the blending mode Soft Light and rename the layer L2D SOFTLIGHT (**Figures 4.14a**, **4.14b**, and **4.14c**).

FIGURE 4.14A *The image map.*

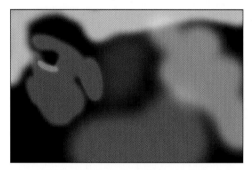

FIGURE 4.14B *What the layer mask looks like.*

FIGURE 4.13 *Before.*

FIGURE 4.14C *After darkening the cheeks, neck, back, and arms by modifying the layer mask of L2D 2 SOFTLIGHT and changing the blending mode from Luminosity to Soft Light.*

FIGURE 4.15A *Sampling the shadow under the model's nose.*

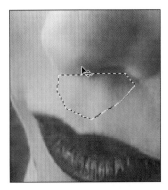 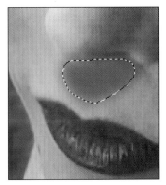

FIGURE 4.15B *Selecting an area under the nose with the Polygonal Lasso tool.*

FIGURE 4.15C *After filling the feathered selection with the foreground shadow color.*

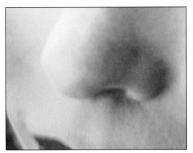

FIGURE 4.15D *Lowering the shadow layer's opacity helps create a natural-looking shadow.*

NOTE: According to Adobe, the blending mode Soft Light "darkens or lightens the colors, depending on the blend color. The effect is similar to shining a diffused spotlight on the image." This means that if the blend color (the light source) is lighter than 50% gray, the image becomes lightened as if it were dodged. If the blend color is darker than 50% gray, the image becomes darkened as if it were burned in. Painting with pure black or white produces a distinctly darker or lighter area, but does not result in pure black or white.

12. Do "The Move," name this layer MASTER LIGHT 1, and save the file.

Step 7: Adding a Butterfly Shadow

When adding shadowing to images, it's a common mistake to not take into account the color of the shadow.

NOTE: See also "Creating a Realistic Shadow," in Chapter 1.

1. Zoom in on the area of the nose and mouth. With the eyedropper, sample the color of the shadow just below the nose (**Figure 4.15a**). The foreground color now reflects the color of the shadow.

2. Create a new layer. With the Polygonal Lasso, make a selection like the one shown, and feather it by 5 pixels. The marching-ants selection border indicates the pixels that are at least 50% selected. Fill the selection with the foreground color (**Figures 4.15b** and **4.15c**).

3. Apply 5.3 pixels of Gaussian blur. Create a layer mask and brush around the shadow with a 40-pixel brush until you are happy with the size. (Remember to use the edge of the brush.) Now, reduce the opacity of the layer until it looks realistic; 15% is about right (**Figure 4.15d**).

The Die Is Cast

Gone is the day that the movie moguls taught actors the importance of posing all day for a photograph.

— George Hurrell

We have now reached the conclusion of this chapter's main focus, creating classic glamour lighting using Photoshop (**Figures 4.16a** and **4.16b**). In the next chapter, you will convert the newly lit *Stardust* image into a continuous-tone black-and-white photograph that has the look and feel of an image captured with film.

FIGURE 4.16A *The original capture.*

Figure 4.16b *The final image.*

Seattle Sequence[4]

Breath of a Dancer²

American Graffiti

Forest from the Trees

Seattle Sequence[6]

Hell of a Place to Loose a Cow

Fog Rise: North Gate

Yes And . . .

Sentinel of the Mist

Fog Rise: Cades Cove

From a Grain of Sand

The Girl Next Door

Seattle Sequence[3]

Tousled Hair

Figure 5.1

Figure 5.2

Chapter 5

Creating a Black-and-White Image from an RGB File

I eagerly await new concepts and processes. I believe that the electronic image will be the next major advance. Such systems will have their own inherent and inescapable structural characteristics, and the artist and functional practitioner will again strive to comprehend and control them.

—Ansel Adams

In this chapter, I'll show you approaches for converting a digitally captured or scanned RGB color file into a continuous-tone black-and-white file that replicates the way black-and-white film would have recorded the image—without ever leaving the RGB color space.

The Soul of Art Photography

For me, the black-and-white image has always been the core, the essence, and the soul of photography. It's almost as if there is more honesty in a black-and-white print than there is in a color one. In a color print, you're never sure if the color you see is the color the photographer saw. Black-and-white reveals the truth of subtle shade and tonal shifts. It has a simplicity, elegance, and beauty that defy description.

The magic in watching a black-and-white image appear in the developer tray, along with the smell of stop bath and fixer, is what sparked my desire to be a photographer. My formal education in photography was in large-format black-and-white nature photography. Before 1998, the year I went totally digital, I was shooting some 6000 rolls of film per year, of which 90% were black-and-white. At the time, I made my living doing head shots for Hollywood actors, and those were always shot and printed in black-and-white.

When I started beta-testing some digital photography equipment in 1992, I was told I had to start shooting color if I wanted to be a beta site for any future devices. So, of course, that's what I did. What surprises me is that I'm now better known for my color images than for my black-and-white ones. No matter; black-and-white remains my first love.

As I entered the digital world, black-and-white prints took a backseat to the new art of digitally capturing color images and to the concerns of how to best produce a print that remained true to my vision. One of the basic tenets of my training as a photographer was derived from an Ansel Adams quote: "The negative is everything, the print is all. The negative is the sheet music and the print is the symphony." That is, the print is the culmination of the effort, the thing you can show to others and sell.

A World of Shadows

In the film world, to make a print worthy of showing to others, you must have a worthy negative. In the digital world, the negative is a file. That file has to contain quality information, or the print that you create from it will be poor. Without good sheet music, the symphony will be worthless.

But what if you have great sheet music, but can no longer create a great symphony from it? Until recently, this was the sorry state of affairs that existed for the great black-and-white negatives produced by such photographic icons as Ansel Adams, Minor White, Edward Weston, and Wynn Bullock. Their prints—the ones with which we fell in love—were made on papers that are no longer available. Today's photographic papers no longer contain heavy metals like cadmium and mercury. OSHA and the EPA have ordered them removed for environmentally sound, but not necessarily aesthetically good, reasons.

Ironically, these same heavy metals made the older papers archivally stable and gave them great maximum densities. Today, when it comes to silver printing, you can achieve a similar result using selenium-toned papers to regain image stability and maximum density.

Also, the photographic papers commercially available today contain less silver than they once did. Unless you're willing to invest the time and expense to create platinum or other alternative-process prints, it's very hard to capture the subtleties and full range of tones within a black-and-white negative on commercially available, silver-based photographic paper. That's the bad news. The good news is that digital cameras, software, and inkjet printing technologies let us create black-and-white prints in ways we no longer thought were possible.

A black-and-white print isn't purely black and white; it's made up of monochromatic tones. Many variables affect the final tone of a black-and-white print. For one thing, each type of silver-based paper produces a print with a characteristic tone. For example, Agfa Insignia, Agfa Portriga, and Forté Salon are warm-tone papers. Oriental Seagull, Agfa Brovira, and Ilford Galerie are cool- to cold-tone papers. Different developers and developer concentrations can also change a print's tone, as can selenium toning.

In the old days, when we were printing on silver-based papers, we chose a particular one and processed it in our individual way in order to achieve a specific tonality that only we could achieve in our secret darkroom dance. We wanted to make a warm- or cold-toned print with rich, deep blacks, detail in the textured blacks or deep shadows, and crisp, textured whites in the highlights. We wanted a print that had a complete tonal range from dark black to pure white, and that goal hasn't changed.

Learning the R-G-Bs

Now that I've defined what's desirable in the print—the type of symphony you want to create—let's look at what constitutes a black-and-white capture on film, and which of its characteristics you want to replicate. It's time to learn how the sheet music is written.

Panchromatic black-and-white film (*pan* means "all" and *chromatic* means "colors") is the film type that is most often used to take black-and-white photographs, because it records light in the range visible to the human eye. Visible light, which is measured in nanometers (nm), is in the 400–700 nm range. A general approximation is that blue ranges from 400 to 500 nm, green from 500 to 600 nm, and red from 600 to 700 nm. The human eye is most sensitive at 555 nm, right in the middle of the green spectrum.

When the mix of colors (or relationship between colors of light) changes, film can record that change. When you enter the digital world, things are different. Digital cameras record the relationships among red, green, and blue light within the image. Red, green, and blue are words used to describe three independent wavelengths of light. Any color that you capture with a digital camera can be defined by its mixture of red (R), green (G), and blue (B) light, and by its profile.

Without explicit reference to an RGB profile—such as Adobe RGB (1998), for example—RGB is meaningless; you simply have no idea what the colors really are. Without a reference RGB profile, all you know is that the red is some shade of red and the green is some shade of green. With a reference RGB profile, you know what those particular shades are.

Film works with density and digital cameras work with luminance, so they have different RGB responses and tone-reproduction curves. Images captured on film will look different from those captured with a digital camera.

Images captured with digital cameras produce digital values relative to the scene luminance as automatically calculated by the camera's tone-reproduction curve. This means that equal changes in scene brightness will produce equal changes in digital values.

Black-and-white film has the ability to record the ever-changing relationship of visible light, and digital cameras record the relationships among R, G, and B. Therefore, it's critical to maintain that relationship when converting a digitally captured image from color (**Figure 5.1**) to black-and-white (**Figure 5.2**) if you want to replicate the look and feel of traditional black-and-white film photography. Bear this in mind when post-processing digital camera images in Photoshop to achieve the look of a classic black-and-white image.

RGB Isn't a Color, It's a Formula to Mix Color

Another factor to consider is that film, digital cameras, and people all see the colors in a scene differently. There are many reasons for this, but two of the more significant ones are the spectral sensitivities and tone-reproduction curves that are unique to each medium. Every film type has unique RGB characteristics because of its photographic emulsion chemistry. Each digital camera type has unique RGB responses and tone-reproduction characteristics because of its RGB sensors and filters, as well as its signal (image) processing characteristics.

Neither film nor digital cameras reproduce color the way the human eye sees it. The eye has unique color and tone responses. Film and digital cameras attempt to approximate the way people see color; but, as is always the case, there are design trade-offs that compromise this goal.

So what is RGB, really? If you walk away from this lesson having learned only one thing—aside from how to make a great black-and-white print from a color capture—it should be this: RGB isn't a color, it's a formula to mix color.

Go to the Channels palette in Photoshop. You will see four channels: RGB, Red, Green, and Blue. If you look at the Red, Green, and Blue channels individually, what you will see is not color, but gray. You will also see that each of these channels yields different intensities of the grayscale for each color in each area of the picture (**Figures 5.3**, **5.4**, **5.5**, and **5.6**).

Figure 5.3 *All channels.*

Figure 5.4 *Red channel.*

FIGURE 5.5 *Green channel.*

FIGURE 5.6 *Blue channel.*

NOTE: The keyboard shortcuts for seeing the Red, Green, and Blue channels individually, as well as the one that shows all three, are: Red: Ctrl-/Cmd-1, Green: Ctrl-/Cmd-2, Blue: Ctrl-/Cmd-3, and to see all the channels at once (or RGB, as it is referred to in the Channels palette): Ctrl-/Cmd-~.

Two Ways Not *to Convert RGB to Black-and-White*

Before you do this lesson, I invite you to experiment and try creating a black-and-white image in the following two ways.

First, globally desaturate the image with Image > Adjustments > Desaturate, then look at the three channels separately. (See above note on how to do this.) You won't see any difference in the image, and when you turn on all three channels, all you will see is a slightly denser image. This approach destroys two-thirds of the spectral relationship and wipes out the relationships among red, green, and blue.

Second, do a "classic" black-and-white conversion. Go to Image > Mode and convert the image from RGB to LAB color mode. Then go to the Channels palette, and throw away the A and B channels. Go back to Mode, convert the image from LAB to grayscale, then go to Mode again and convert the image from grayscale to RGB. Now, look at the Red, Green, and Blue channels. Again, there is no change. Basically, you have duplicated the luminance channel three times, and again destroyed two-thirds of the relational spectral data, albeit to a lesser degree.

These two approaches produce digital black-and-white prints in which some element of visual richness is missing. Those missing elements are the spectral relationships among R, G, and B. Preserving those relationships is the aim of the three conversion methods I will discuss next.

Basic Black-and-White Conversion

FIGURE 5.7

FIGURE 5.8

Step 1: Create a Hue/Saturation Adjustment Layer

1. On the disc that accompanies this book, go to the folder BW 1, and open the file STARDUST 1 SOURCE.TIFF.

2. Create a Hue/Saturation adjustment layer, and move the Saturation slider to 100%. Generally, this is the first step I take to analyze color. By increasing the saturation, you exaggerate the differences between the colors in the image, making it easy to see which are dominant. The areas that posterize tend to be the areas that will present the greatest difficulty (**Figure 5.7**).

Notice that the colors are very skewed to the yellows and reds. Knowing which colors dominate will help you decide how to adjust the Channel Mixer layers or additional Hue/Saturation layers for the final compensation adjustments, which you will see in Step 6.

Step 2: Sample the Highlights

1. Using the Color Sampler tool, make sample points of all the highlight areas. You do this by Shift-clicking the area you want to sample and releasing the mouse. This creates a set of reference points to help ensure that you don't blow out the highlight areas during the conversion to black-and-white.

To spot potential trouble areas, look for extreme color posterization where smooth color gradations turn contrasty and saturated. Posterization usually occurs in areas where highlights are in danger of being blown out. In this image, there are four main areas of concern. Position 1 is the highlight area on the subject's side, position 2 is on the subject's lower leg, position 3 is on her forehead, and position 4 is on the upper part of her hair (**Figure 5.8**).

NOTE: In digital capture, if you blow out a highlight, the data is forever lost. Shadows are a different story; depending on your ISO you have upwards of two f-stops of latitude. Which means, in theory, that you can recover upwards of two stops of data when you process the raw file in what ever digital RAW-processing software you use, or in Photoshop. The best way to do this in Photoshop is to use a Curves adjustment layer.

In the Info palette, you will see the numerical level values of Red, Green, and Blue for each sample point (**Figure 5.9**).

FIGURE 5.9

FIGURE 5.10   FIGURE 5.10A

Watch those values during the conversion, and make sure none exceeds 244–247. I generally aim for 95% saturation, or a value of 242 (+/− 2), so that the detailed highlights aren't blocked up. Specular highlights or pure paper white can go up to 255, of course.

NOTE: In the Zone System, 244–247 corresponds to Zone IX, textured white. Detailed shadows are Zone II. The goal is to hit 244, but with wiggle room up to 247. The risk of losing detail in the highlights increases as you get closer to 255, which corresponds to no data at all—the white of the paper.

2. When the sample points are set, bring the saturation back to 0, and click OK.

Like Zone II textured blacks or detailed shadows, Zone IX detailed highlights make an image interesting to the eye by giving it visual richness. They are also are the hallmark of a technically proficient printer in both the silver and silicon worlds of photography. As Ansel Adams said, "All the great photographers in the world are great printers. But every great printer is not necessarily a great photographer."

Step 3: The First Channel Mixer Adjustment Layer

1. Create the first Channel Mixer adjustment layer, and select Green from the Output Channel menu. You will see Red and Blue at 0%, Green at +100%, and the Constant at 0%. Now click Monochrome. Two things just happened. The image went to grayscale and the output channel changed from Green to Gray. Also notice that the Red and Blue channels are still at 0% and the Green channel is at +100% (**Figures 5.10** and **5.10a**).

NOTE: When you first enter the Channel Mixer layer, Photoshop defaults to the Red output channel, but when you're creating a black-and-white image to be printed, it's best to start with Green. The Green channel generally contains more information about relative brightness in the image than the Red or Blue channels. Those contain information about relative contrast in the image, so they should be used to darken or lighten specific areas.

Adjust the Red, Green, Blue, and Constant sliders to create an image with appealing midtone values without blowing out the highlights, blocking up the shadows, or flattening the image with an overall gray cast. I chose +5% Red, +80% Green, and +24% Blue, with the Constant at 2% (**Figures 5.11** and **5.12**).

The Constant slider adds a black or white channel of varying opacity. When it is negative, it acts as a black channel, and when it is positive, it acts as a white one. Its effect is to either globally darken with negative values or globally lighten with positive ones. In other words, it increases (adding black) or decreases (adding white) the density of the Channel Mixer adjustment layer. You often get a relationship of Red to Green to Blue that you find appealing, but find that the highlights are blown out or the deep shadows are too dark. The Constant slider lets you compensate for this. It's tricky to use, however, and the latitude of compensation it gives is never more than plus or minus 10%.

2. Click OK and name the layer GREEN.

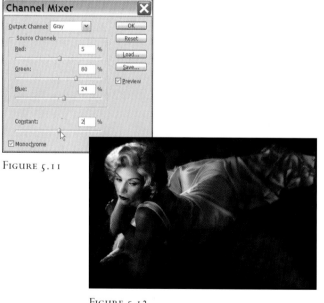

FIGURE 5.11

FIGURE 5.12

Some people believe that when working with the Channel Mixer, the sum of the Red, Green, Blue, and constant values must always add up to 100. However, when doing a black-and-white conversion using the method described in this chapter, you will find that the sum of the numbers will range anywhere from the high 80s to the low 130s. Generally, the RGB values add up to around 100, but not always. So rather than try to match some arbitrary number, depend on your built-in spectrophotometer, densitometer, and colorimeter; your eyes.

Step 4: The Second Channel Mixer Adjustment Layer

1. Create a second Channel Mixer adjustment layer on top of the layer named GREEN, and click Monochrome. Photoshop defaults to Red, the next color channel you will manipulate. Your eye sees red less efficiently than green, but more efficiently than blue. You should see Red at +100%, Green and Blue at 0%, and the Constant at 0%.

2. Set the Channel Mixer layer settings for this adjustment to +90% Red, +8% Green, and +8% Blue, with the Constant at −6%. Click OK and name this layer RED (**Figures 5.13** and **5.14**).

Step 5: The Third Channel Mixer Adjustment Layer

1. Create a third Channel Mixer adjustment layer on top of the layer named RED, select the Blue channel, then click Monochrome.

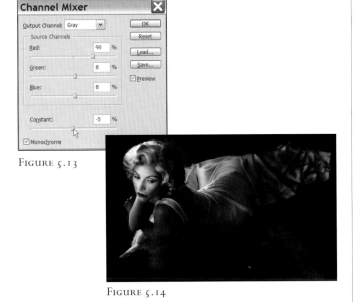

FIGURE 5.13

FIGURE 5.14

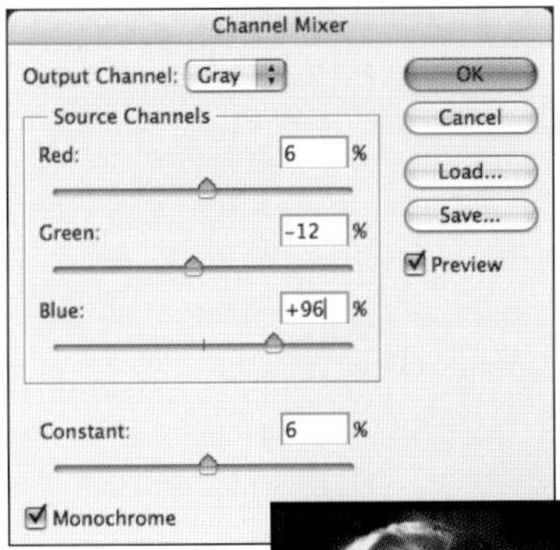

You should see Red and Green at 0%, Blue at +100%, and the Constant at 0%. Watch the numerical values in the Info palette as you adjust this Channel Mixer layer.

2. For this image, I chose +6% Red, −12% Green, and +96% Blue, with the Constant at 6%. Click OK, and name this layer BLUE (**Figures 5.15**, **5.16**, **5.17**, **5.18**, and **5.19**).

FIGURE 5.17 *Red Channel Mixer layer.*

FIGURE 5.18 *Green Channel Mixer layer.*

FIGURE 5.15

FIGURE 5.16 *All Channel Mixer layers.*

FIGURE 5.19 *Blue Channel Mixer layer.*

FIGURE 5.20

FIGURE 5.21

It's important to observe that the Red Channel Mixer layer is almost identical to the Red channel before you did anything. The same holds true for the Green and Blue Channel Mixer layers. What you have just done preserves the spectral relationships among R, G, and B in the same manner that they would have been recorded if the image had been shot on black-and-white film. Also note that on the Info palette, the value of sample point 4 is 245.

Step 6: Adjust the Saturation

Now you are going to revisit the observations made when you brought the saturation to 100%. Specifically, you will address the issues that arose in the conversion to black-and-white.

The first issue to address is the color of the woman's lips. By starting the conversion with the Green channel—which is like putting a green filter over a lens and photographing something red with black-and-white film—the red lipstick turned black. You can address this by adjusting the saturation and lightness of the reds and selectively varying the amount of the adjustment by using the layer mask in the Hue/Saturation adjustment layer.

1. Make active the Hue/Saturation adjustment layer that you created in Step 1, and double-click the layer thumbnail to open the Hue/Saturation dialog. Select Reds from the Edit menu, and move the Saturation and Lightness sliders to produce acceptable tonality in the lips. I chose saturation –58 and lightness +58 (**Figures 5.20** and **5.21**).

2. Click OK to close the dialog.

This dealt with the issue of the lips and to some degree the skin tone, but it also lightened the entire image. You will correct this by painting on the adjustment layer's layer mask.

FIGURE 5.22

FIGURE 5.23

FIGURE 5.24

3. Fill the adjustment layer's layer mask with black, and make sure the foreground color is white and the background color black. (Shortcut: To set the foreground and background colors to their default colors, press D.) With a soft, 150-pixel brush at 50% opacity, paint the face, arms, and back. After all these areas have been brushed, reduce the brush diameter to 50 pixels. Now paint in the lips. When that's done, lower the opacity of the adjustment layer itself to 65% (**Figures 5.22**, **5.23**, and **5.24**).

You have just completed a basic black-and-white conversion. Now let's raise the bar a bit and try something a little more difficult. The next two conversion methods are more advanced, but they yield even greater control of the relationships among R, G, and B.

In the first, you will change the order of the layers and use the Channel Mixer adjustment layer masks for selective control. In the second, you will use the fourth Channel Mixer layer to expand the dynamic range of a continuous-tone, black-and-white RGB file.

Advanced B/W Conversion No. 1

Changing the Layer Order and Using Channel Mixer Adjustment Layer Masks for Selective Control

You have a choice: you can do the conversion yourself, by following the steps learned above in the basic black-and-white lesson (use the file STARDUST 2 BASE.tif), or you can use the converted file provided (STARDUST 2 CONVERTED.psd). To see the effect, see **Figures 5.25** and **5.26**.

If you choose to do the basic black-and-white conversion, follow these steps, which were discussed above:

1. Analyze the image using a Hue/Saturation adjustment layer.
2. Note the major color components.
3. Place sample points on the potential highlight problem areas. (Look at the areas of posterization to find them.)

4. Determine what potential highlight problem areas are the most important and make your decisions about how to "mix" the individual channels with them in mind.
5. Create a Channel Mixer adjustment layer, select Green from the Output Channel menu, then click Monochrome.
6. Modify the sliders until the image looks appealing. Click OK and name the layer GREEN.
7. Repeat Steps 5 and 6 for the Red channel, then the Blue channel.
8. Make any final adjustments using a Hue/Saturation adjustment layer and an appropriate mask. (This is always the last step of the conversion process. Even after changing the layer order, which I'm about to cover.)

NOTE: If you get stumped, you can open either layered files STARDUST 2 AWB 100PPI.psd or STARDUST AWB 100PPI.psd and look at the numbers for reference.

FIGURE 5.25 *The original color* Stardust *image.*

FIGURE 5.26 *After conversion to black and white.*

FIGURE 5.27 *Green.*   FIGURE 5.28 *Red.*

Step 1: Changing Channel Mixer Layer Order

1. Turn on just the Green Channel Mixer layer, then the Red, and finally the Blue. Observe what they look like.

Green has the most midtone information, Red is the lightest, and Blue is the darkest. The skin tone in the Red channel is the smoothest, but it lacks the detail of the Green channel (**Figures 5.27**, **5.28**, and **5.29**).

2. Turn on all the Channel Mixer adjustment layers. Make the RED layer active and move it beneath the Green Channel Mixer layer, so the layer order from the bottom up is RED, GREEN, BLUE (**Figure 5.30**).

3. Now move the Blue Channel Mixer adjustment layer beneath the Red, so the layer order from the bottom up is now BLUE, RED, GREEN (**Figure 5.31**).

FIGURE 5.29 *Blue.*

FIGURE 5.30   FIGURE 5.31

FIGURE 5.32 *Green channel, before.*

FIGURE 5.33 *Image map.*

FIGURE 5.34 *After.*

Compare what you observed in the individual Channel Mixer layers with what you observe when you change their order. The overall image looks best in the Red channel but lacks depth. Green has the most midtone data but doesn't have as nice a "feel" to the skin tones as the Red. Blue is what it is, the darkest, or densest, of the three Channel Mixer layers, with the least amount of detail. So each channel has something that the others lack. When you lead with Red, the face blows out, but the overall quality of the image improves. When you lead with Blue, the image isn't affected. This is important because, since all three channels are different, you will see a marked alteration when you change the order of the Red and Green channels. If you want to see more expression of the Blue Channel Mixer layer, you will have to do brushwork on the Red and Green layer masks, no matter what their order.

One of the advantages of adjustment layers is that they all come with layer masks, remember? So you will use layer masks to correct the problems we created by changing the Channel Mixer layer order.

You need to tone down aspects of the Green channel so that there is a greater Red-to-Green relationship in some areas. In those same areas, you need to tone down the Red channel so that there is a greater Green-to-Red relationship, as well as a greater Blue-to-Red-to-Green relationship. This means that there are areas of both the Red and Green Channel Mixer layers that need brushwork to allow the influence of the Blue Channel Mixer to be expressed.

This may appear complicated, but it's actually quite simple. Just keep in mind that even though the image has the appearance of a continuous-tone black-and-white one, it's still a color image. Remember, RGB isn't a color; it's a formula to mix color.

Step 2: Using Layer Masks with the Channel Mixer Adjustment Layers

You want the face to use just the RED and BLUE adjustment layers, and aspects of the background to use RED rather than GREEN and BLUE.

FIGURE 5.35 *Red channel, before.*

FIGURE 5.36 *Image map.*

1. Start with the Green Channel Mixer adjustment layer, because green is the color that carries luminance and the mid-tone detail. Do the brushwork suggested by the image map (**Figures 5.32**, **5.33**, and **5.34**).

2. Now make the Red Channel Mixer layer the active layer. Notice that the bear's nose is completely blown out, that the model's face and hair are a little too "glowy" and flat, and that the back of her gown is a little glowy as well. This is what an image map of the red Channel looks like. The image now looks like this (**Figures 5.35**, **5.36**, and **5.37**).

FIGURE 5.37 *After.*

Advanced B/W Conversion No. 2

The Fourth Channel Mixer Layer: Expanding the Dynamic Range of a Continuous-Tone Black-and-White RGB File

At this point you should be fairly clear on the concept that red, green, and blue, the primary colors of light, all have relationships with each other. It's that interrelationship in the visible spectrum that our eye perceives as "color." What is unique about black-and-white film is its ability to record the spectral relationships among the primaries of light; it can also record the changes in those spectral relationships and do so in a grayscale.

When you convert RGB to a "gray scale" the way you did in the previous two exercises, you basically created a "digital positive negative." Negative in the sense that, just like a film negative, it's the base representation of the photographed experience, warts and all. Positive in the negative-to-print sense, because what we are seeing is what the print would look like if we printed it. The negative is everything. It is the sheet music.

In the next exercise, you are going to create an RGB image with a grayscale tonal range, and then dramatically expand that tonal range without ever leaving the RGB color space. This will be the equivalent of developing a traditional, silver, black-and-white print with a two-step development process.

Figure 5.38   Figure 5.39

Step 1: Controlling the Relationship of Red to Green to Blue after Primary Black-and-White Conversion of an RGB File to Extend Tonal Range

1. On the disc, find the picture of the man with the pipe called BEFORE.TIFF, and do the same kind of basic, three-Channel Mixer, black-and-white conversion that you did in the first exercise. Or, if you prefer, you can use the already converted file ABW 3 CONVERTED.PSD (**Figures 5.38** and **5.39**).

2. Just as in the first advanced conversion approach, look at the image with each of the Channel Mixer adjustment layers visible, first one at a time, then all three together (**Figures 5.40**, **5.41**, **5.42**, and **5.43**).

3. Make the Red layer active and move it beneath the Green Channel Mixer layer, so the layer order from the bottom up is RED, GREEN, BLUE (**Figure 5.44**).

4. Now move the Blue Channel Mixer adjustment layer beneath the Red, so that the layer order from the bottom up is now BLUE, RED, GREEN.

FIGURE 5.40 *Green layer.*

FIGURE 5.41 *Red layer.*

FIGURE 5.42 *Blue layer.*

FIGURE 5.43 *All Channel Mixer layers.*

FIGURE 5.44

Looking at the image this way, you can see it with all its desirable and undesirable parts. As with the image of the model on the bearskin, leading with the Red Channel Mixer gives the best overall image, but it wreaks havoc on the man's face. It's always best to start with Green, go to Red second, and to Blue third. Only after you have an acceptable base image should you start to correct the rough spots. No two images are the same, and no two black-and-white conversions are, either. Workflow is dynamic, not dogmatic.

Doing the Developer Two-Step

In classic black-and-white printing, one of the best ways to extend the tonal range of a silver print was to split the development process into two steps. You could also do this with the negative, but I found that splitting the print development gave me a better result. The primary reason for this was that it gave me better control; I could see what was happening and therefore had better control of the outcome. The process involved using two developer solutions: Solution A—a metol developing bath, and Solution B—a hydroquinone developing bath. By varying the times in these two development baths, you could extend or contract the dynamic range by at least one entire paper grade. By varying the proportions of metol and hydroquinone, a developer could yield either low contrast (more metol, less hydroquinone) or high contrast (less metol, more hydroquinone). The process was unwieldy and inconsistent (for example, the developer exhausted itself very quickly), but it produced superior prints.

FIGURE 5.45 *Green before.*

FIGURE 5.46 *Image map.*

FIGURE 5.47 *After.*

NOTE: As a rule, I find that putting the Green Channel Mixer adjustment layer first (working from the bottom up) looks the best 80 percent of the time, Red 15%, and Blue 5%.

The image has two specific problems: (1) The red aspect of the conversion must be balanced for the skin, and (2) The contrast on the man's shirt must be flattened. Because of this, you will be working with all three Channel Mixer layers, as well as their masks. So what you need is a little insurance.

1. Create a Channel Mixer layer, select Monochrome, and type 33 into each of the Red, Green, and Blue dialog boxes. Type 1 in the Constant box.

2. Click OK and name this layer NEUTRAL.

What you just did created a neutralizing layer. The presence of this layer guarantees that no color will bleed through should there be any brush overlap on the individual Channel Mixer layers' masks.

NOTE: If all you're going to do is change the layer order, or work on one or two of the three layers, you don't need to create this fourth layer. It's only necessary if you are going to work on all three layers, as you will do in this exercise. If you create this fourth layer, it must be the topmost Channel Mixer layer.

3. Make GREEN the active layer. You want more red than green in the mix to give a smoother skin tone. Make the foreground color black, select a brush at 50% opacity, and brush in the areas shown on the image map (**Figures 5.45**, **5.46**, and **5.47**).

4. Make RED the active layer. Select the Brush tool, make the foreground color black, and set the opacity to 50%. Brush in the areas shown on the image map (**Figures 5.48**, **5.49**, and **5.50**).

5. Make BLUE the active layer. Select the Brush tool, make the foreground color black, and set the opacity to 50%. Brush in the areas following the image map (**Figures 5.51**, **5.52**, and **5.53**).

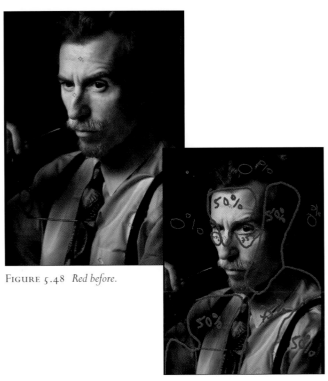

FIGURE 5.48 *Red before.*

FIGURE 5.49 *Image map.*

FIGURE 5.51 *Blue before.*

FIGURE 5.52 *Image map.*

FIGURE 5.50 *After.*

FIGURE 5.53 *After.*

FIGURE 5.54 *The image after brushwork in all three channels.*

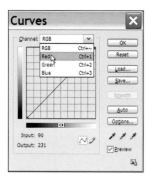

FIGURE 5.55

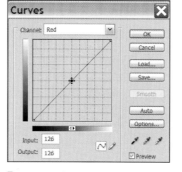

FIGURE 5.56

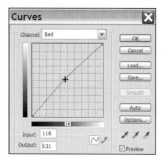

FIGURE 5.57

FIGURE 5.58

Look at the image after you have done the brushwork in all three channels (**Figure 5.54**).

6. Make NEUTRAL the active layer. Create a master layer, and name it MASTER 1.

7. Save the file as a Photoshop file (.psd), and name it STEVE B&W.PSD.

NOTE: To see the purpose of the NEUTRAL layer, toggle it on and off, and notice color bleed where the brush strokes on the masks overlapped.

Step 2: Adding Tonality

In traditional silver black-and-white photography, a purely neutral black-and-white print does not really exist. All traditionally made prints, be they silver or platinum, have some degree of color produced by the reaction between the chemicals used in the developing process and the very color of the paper itself. Some people prefer cooler, bluer tones. Personally, I prefer a warm tone for both portraits and landscapes, so I will show you how to create a warm tonality using Curves and Hue/Saturation adjustment layers. You can use the same approach to make a cool-tone image as well.

1. Create a Curves adjustment layer. From the Channel pulldown menu, select Red. Click the center point of the curve, creating an anchor point (**Figures 5.55** and **5.56**).

2. With the arrow keys, move the curve upward to increase the red content. You can move the anchor point from side to side as well as back down. What I came up with for the red aspect of my tonality was this curve and image (**Figures 5.57** and **5.58**).

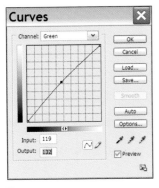

FIGURE 5.59

FIGURE 5.60

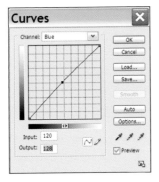

FIGURE 5.61

FIGURE 5.62 *Before adding tonality.* FIGURE 5.63 *After adding tonality.*

3. Do the same thing in the Green channel, producing this curve and image (**Figures 5.59** and **5.60**).

4. Lastly, do the same in the Blue channel, producing this curve (**Figure 5.61**).

5. Click OK and name this Curve adjustment layer WARM CURVE (**Figures 5.62** and **5.63**).

6. Create a Hue/Saturation adjustment layer. Select Colorize. You should see a dialog and image that look like this (**Figures 5.64** and **5.65**).

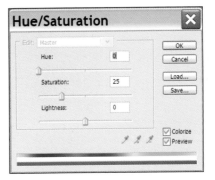

FIGURE 5.64

FIGURE 5.65

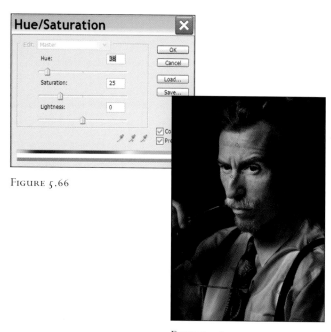

FIGURE 5.66

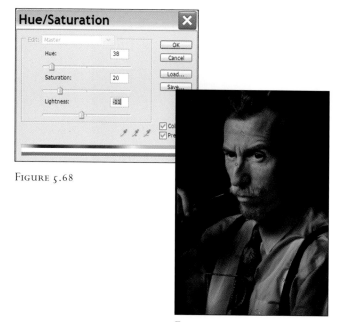

FIGURE 5.68

FIGURE 5.67

7. Move the Hue slider to the right. The image will start to change color. I stopped at a hue of 38 (**Figures 5.66** and **5.67**).

Hue, in the Hue/Saturation adjustment layer, is a linearized color wheel. If you move the Hue slider completely from side to side, you will notice that when the slider is all the way to the right or to the left, the color of the image is exactly the same.

Lower the saturation to 20 and the lightness to −11 (**Figures 5.68** and **5.69**).

8. Click OK. Name this layer WARM HUE.

All the decisions concerning hue, saturation, and lightness are purely a matter of personal taste. You may like something different from the choices I made here. The trick is to focus on getting the overall tone right. Then you can use layer opacity to dial in the desired intensity.

9. I chose to lower the WARM HUE layer opacity to 25% and the WARM CURVE layer opacity to 50%, producing this image (**Figure 5.70**).

10. Make the WARM HUE layer active. Use Cmd-Option-Shift-E/Ctrl-Alt-Shift-E to make a copy of all visible layers and then merge them into a new master layer, name it MASTER 2, and save the file.

FIGURE 5.70 *Conversion completed.*

FIGURE 5.69

From Oz to Kansas

In this approach, I chose to use both Curves and Hue/Saturation adjustment layers, because neither is as finely tunable as I would like it to be. But between the two, you can mix the colors the way you want them, and by lowering the opacity, you can get the intensity you want. Remember, RGB isn't a color; it's a formula for mixing color. As you have learned in previous chapters, gray is a color in the RGB world. Even shadows that appear to be gray are anything but. Therefore, when you create an image that replicates the reality of a traditionally printed black-and-white print, the grays and blacks have to be assigned a color and tone.

This has not been an easy lesson. Consider, however, that it took me eight years to develop these techniques. But while this chapter may be the hardest to grasp, it is the one that best shows the power of approaching RGB as a formula for mixing color, and that anything you see has color, even when that color is gray. This concept holds true for any work you do on an image, from capture to image manipulation to output. So don't give up if you don't get it right immediately. All it takes is a little time and practice. Practice doesn't make perfect, *perfect* practice makes perfect.

FIGURE 6.1A

FIGURE 6.1B *Time and movement in the water of the San Francisco Bay:* Smoke.

Chapter 6

It's About Time

Ever notice that people will measure distance in time, but not time in distance?
If you ask someone how far away they are from work, they say,
"Oh, about 15 minutes." But if you ask them when they get off work,
they never say, "Oh, about a mile and a half."

—Jerry Seinfeld

In this final chapter, we are going to explore the most elusive thing in photography; placing the experience of time in a photograph. This is the last, rather than the first chapter of this book, because before you could create such an image, you had to understand all the parts that would eventually go to make up the whole.

Capturing the Moment

The human being can assess his circumstances and judge his limitations within those circumstances, all through a mental programming, never risking his flesh until an optimum course has been computed. The human being may do this within the compression of elapsed time so short, it may be called instantaneous.

—Frank Herbert

I have covered a lot of territory up to this point. So I'm going to review some of the things that I have discussed in previous chapters.

- A still photograph is called a still photograph because the picture doesn't move, not because the objects in the picture were not in motion at the time of capture.
- Visualize the finished image in your mind's eye as you are taking the picture. Do not go out with a camera with preconceived notions of what you will capture; you want to be open to possibilities.
- Get it right in the camera. If it doesn't look good through the lens, it will not look good coming out of the printer.
- RGB is not a color; it's a formula to mix color.

- If you can see something, it has color. Gray is a color and "black is the queen of all colors."
- "Practice doesn't make perfect. Perfect practice makes perfect. Perfect practice comes from practicing at practicing."
- Workflow starts at the point of capturing the image.
- A believable improbability is better than an improbable believability.
- The more you know about the middle, the more informed your decisions can be at the beginning, because everything you do is in service of the print (the end), and the print is your voice.
- Workflow is a dynamic, not a static, experience. No two images are the same; therefore, no two workflows are the same. Be adaptive: always pro-act rather than react.
- The human eye is an organic optical recording device that can see motion, and a digital still camera cannot.
- Shape is the enemy of color.
- A pattern is interesting, but a pattern interrupted is more interesting.
- If you want the eye to remember color over shape, cause shape to become the unwitting ally of color.

- The viewer looks at a photograph with two "eyes," the unconscious and conscious ones. The conscious eye interprets the image that the unconscious eye (the organic optical recording device) sees.
- The unconscious "sees" in a predictable manner. It first recognizes light areas and then moves to dark ones, sees high before low contrast, records high before low sharpness, notices focus before blur, and focuses on high color saturation before low.
- Consider light a tangible thing, so what you photograph is not the subject, but the light as it falls on the subject.
- The key components of any photograph that I've mentioned thus far are light, gesture, and color.

I want to amend this last statement. I believe that there are *four* key components to any photograph: light, gesture, color, and *the consideration of time*. I believe that you can imbue your photographs with a sense of time if you approach the photographing of the visual experience as capturing motion with stillness, rather than as "freezing the moment." If you can do this, you will create images that evoke the sensation of being between moments.

Time is more than the mere ticking of a clock, and to understand how we express time in a photograph, there are many questions we need to ask ourselves about how we experience time. For example, does time only exist in the "now" moment? Is the "now" moment the only time in which reality exists? Or, as Einstein stated, is reality just an illusion, albeit a persistent one? How long is the present? When do the past and future begin? Perhaps the past is the end of your last breath, and the future the end of the one you are taking now. Pondering these philosophical questions will create in you an awareness of time. It is that awareness that I try to include in every image I create. I know that I have been successful when I look at such an image and feel that it embodies a breath held expectant.

How Long Is Now?

Put your hand on a hot stove for a minute, and it seems like an hour. Sit with a pretty girl for an hour, and it seems like a minute. THAT'S relativity.

—Albert Einstein

Perhaps more than any other form of expression, a still photograph holds heightened memories of what was experienced when the picture was taken. A memory is made up of a series of "nows." Can we capture these? First, you should understand that "now" has whatever meaning you wish it to. Current state-of-the-art digital cameras are capable of shooting at 1/8,000 of a second at a burst rate of 8.5 frames a second. Is that the length of "now"? Or is it even shorter? If the camera were able to shoot at 1/24,000 of a second, a shutter speed fast enough to capture or "stop" the movement of a bullet cutting completely through a playing card, but before the card was cut in two, would that be the length of now?

Whatever "now" is for you, the advent of digital photography made it possible to capture a series of "now" moments (**Figure 6.1a**) that you can combine into one image (**Figure 6.1b**). A photograph thus created is an expression of the experience of time. When we take a photograph, we are trying to capture motion with stillness; something that includes a bit of the past, so that it appears in the present in the final composition. Let's take a look at an image harvested with time as a consideration; the image entitled *Kismet*. When you view this image, your conscious eye sees the fog parting, a shaft of light breaking through and hitting the north tower of the Golden Gate Bridge, and a rainbow (**Figure 6.2a**).

When someone sees this image for the first time, I frequently hear, "I've seen that...but I've never been able to photograph it." Then they tell me that I'm the luckiest photographer in the world for having been at the right spot at the right moment to capture it. In reality, this image is made up of nine images shot over an hour and a half. What actually

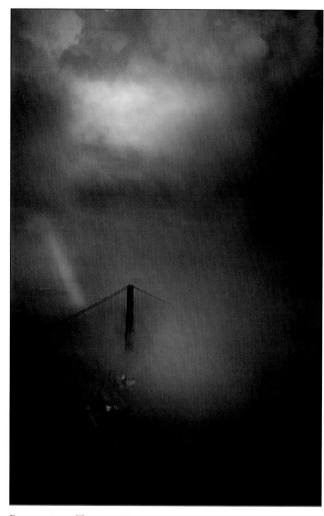

FIGURE 6.2A *The image* Kismet.

happened is that first, the rainbow appeared in a cloudless, fogless sky. Then the ray of light hit the bridge, after which the fog rolled in and the clouds appeared. What I created was an image that reflected all that I experienced during the time that I was shooting (**Figures 6.2b**, **6.2c**, **6.2d**, **6.2e**, **6.2f**, **6.2g**, **6.2h**, and **6.2i**).

What I strive to do in all my photographs, as I have in *Kismet*, is to combine a series of "now" moments into one image that will be seen by the viewer as a single "now." What is so exciting about digital photography combined with Photoshop is that, not only do we have a method of harvesting and holding our experience of time, we can make the past present every time the image is viewed.

The Challenge of Water

The chief enemy of creativity is good sense.

—Pablo Picasso

The captures that comprise the image entitled *Smoke* were shot in the San Francisco Presidio near the old Coast Guard pier. From June 2000 to September 2001, I worked on a photographic project for the Presidio Trust to create a permanent body of art about the historic site. I would often spend time on the old pier watching the sun set over the bay. I never tired of the images created by the ebb and flow of the waves and how they crashed onto the beach. I loved being there, but I couldn't figure out how to capture the feeling of the way the water moved. The issue I have with many images of flowing water—including the ones I've shot myself over the years—is that this moving, fluid thing that you observe over time is often portrayed so statically that the final image has no fluidity at all.

The usual approach to photographing water is to either freeze it or blur it. You can use a fast shutter speed and capture a frozen moment of the water's flow, but the image will not express its movement. Or you can shoot at a slower speed

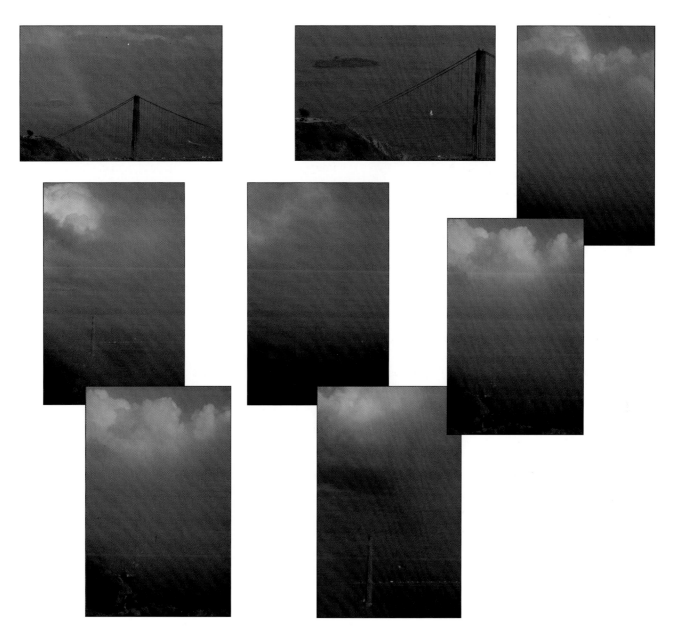

FIGURES 6.02B–I *The* Kismet *source images.*

and get a fluid, smoky image, but you will not capture any detail of the flow or that over which the water moves. Neither image will express the experience of time in a way that matches yours when you saw it.

I finally found that to create an image that conveyed the experience of the ebb and flow of the water, I had to create one image that contained *all* expressions of the water's motion. I accomplished that by image harvesting for each expression and how that changed over time.

It's Graduation Time

Everything should be made as simple as possible, but not simpler.

—Albert Einstein

You will now recreate the image *Smoke*, using all that you have learned in this book. I am going to drop you into the middle of the pixel ocean and you'll have to swim to shore, but I'll be swimming beside you. Most of my instructions will be simply stated, for instance, "Create a master layer, name it MASTER 1,

and save the file." Or, "Create a layer mask, fill it with black, and brush out the areas shown on the image map." See if you can figure out the details of each of the steps you must take. All you will have are the "Before" image, the image map, the "After" image, and the layer mask.

Before you start working on this image, try analyzing it on your own. Begin by asking, Where exactly do I want the unconscious eye to go first, second, third, etc.? What is the pattern that I want recognized first, second, third, and so on? How do I want to control light to dark, high to low contrast, high to low sharpness, and focus to blur? Remember that shape is the enemy of color (even in black-and-white), that gray is a color, and that "black is the queen of all colors." Keep in mind that patterns are interesting, but patterns interrupted are even more interesting, and that light is a tangible thing. Finally, think about how you will place the experience of time in your photograph.

To give you an idea of the work that I put into creating the image *Smoke*, here is the composite of all of my image maps (**Figure 6.3**).

FIGURE 6.3 *The composite of all the image maps used to create* Smoke.

The Flow of *Smoke*

Go to an extreme and retreat to a usable position.

—Brian Eno

The experience of time that I wanted included in this image begins when the wave is crashing and ends when it is about to recede. I am capturing motion with stillness. All of the aesthetic choices that will direct the viewer's unconscious eye, as well as which of the images captured would be used in the final composition, were chosen with that in mind. Knowing what the final picture should look like, let us begin at the beginning.

FIGURE 6.4A *The Smoke base image will be the TEXTURE layer.*

FIGURE 6.4B *This image will be named IN when we make it a layer, because in this capture, the water was moving in.*

FIGURE 6.4C *This image will be named IN/OUT when we make it a layer, because in this capture, the water was moving both in and out.*

Step 1: Combine the Three Images

You'll use elements from three different captures to produce the final image. These are your source files, which you'll find on the disc that accompanies this book. Look in the CH06 folder in the CH06 16 BIT SOURCE FILES folder.

SFDLWS050083.tif
SFDLWS050085.tif
SFDLWS050091.tif

NOTE: This is how the files got their names: SF is the location, as in San Francisco. DLWS is the event—the Digital Landscape Workshop. The digits 05 represent the year that the images were captured, and 83, 85, and 91 are the specific files. As you create your own naming convention, keep it simple and easy to remember. For example, from the file name, I can tell you where and when the image was taken. From the number, I can tell you where each capture was in the shooting sequence.

1. Open the files SFDLWS050083.tif, SFDLWS050085.tif, and SFDLWS050091.tif. I chose SFDLWS050091 as the base image, because it has all the necessary detail in the rocks, but no water (**Figures 6.4a**, **6.4b**, and **6.4c**).

2. Shift-drag the Background layer from SFDLWS050085 onto SFDWLS050091, and name the new layer IN/OUT (for inward/outward flow of the water). Do the same with the Background layer from SFDLWS050083 and name the new layer IN (for the inward flow of the water). Duplicate the Background layer, name this layer TEXTURE, move it atop the layer heap, duplicate it again, and create a layer mask for the layer TEXTURE. Duplicate the IN and OUT layers and create layer masks for them.

NOTE: The three duplicated layers should be together and above the layers from which they were copied.

This lesson, except for the image maps, which were done after the fact, follows my workflow exactly as I did it the first time. What that means is that I wrote this lesson when I first created the image. Where I have changed a step, I will make note of what actually happened. In those instances, I've spared you what I originally did in order to save you time. In other words, in this lesson you will see most of the warts.

The reason I chose to duplicate all the layers was that I knew I was going to build up the depth of the image with multiple versions of my source layers. I was not certain, however, if I was going to use them all. Also, I knew I would need to see what was actually going on in the layer on which I was working. As soon as I filled the layer mask with black, I concealed that layer and saw only the layer beneath. By having a copy of the layer, I could toggle back and forth, by turning the eyeball off and on, to see exactly what was in the layer that I had concealed.

Some image maps were done after the fact, because I knew that this image was going to become a lesson in this book from the first moment that I looked at the captured files in my file browser. So, after I created the amount of detail and opacity that I felt was visually appealing, I went back and mapped it out. This was to ensure that I would have the most accurate representation of what I had done. Remember, the goal of image mapping is to train yourself how to engage in perfect practice by practicing at practicing. It is also a way to record in a visual way what you did.

3. From the bottom, the layer stack order should be Background, OUT, OUT copy, IN, IN copy, TEXTURE, and TEXTURE copy. Turn off everything but the Background and OUT layers. Make the OUT layer active and fill the layer mask with black. "Save As" the file (Shift-Ctrl-S/Shift-Cmd-S) SMOKE 16bit and save it as a Photoshop document (.PSD).

NOTE: Be sure to close the original source files. Once you have shift dragged them into one document, you no longer need them.

Next, decide which are your biggest problems. Then work from global to granular to address them. The biggest issue you face is creating one image. As you do this, you should consider the choices you will make regarding high-to-low contrast, high-to-low sharpness, and in-focus-to-blur. Your choices should be made so that shape becomes the unwitting ally of color and so that you include an expression of time.

You have duplicated all of the layers and their layer masks because, as you have seen in the two lighting lessons, by alternating layers of sharper, more defined images (those with high-to-low sharpness) with those that are in focus but contain blur, you can create an illusion of depth.

4. Make the IN/OUT layer active. Fill the layer mask with black, and brush in the water. My choices for brushing were based on the light-to-dark decisions that I made when I created the first set of image maps.

NOTE: You don't have to map out the image all at once. You can build up the image maps the same way you build the image, in layers. Image maps are a way to teach yourself how to organize an image in a visual way. The goal is to practice at practicing to the point where you will be able to work on an image without using them.

To this point, all the changes I have made to the image *Smoke* were based on where I wanted the observer's eye to go. Thus, on the IN/OUT image map, I reinforced light-to-dark and in-focus-to-blur. The IN/OUT layer was the first on which I did brushwork, because the peak of the wave's crash, just before the wave recedes, was to be the main subject of the image. Therefore, the water's outward movement is what I wanted as the undertone upon which I would build. The base layer was the one with no water, so that I could work additively. It is easier to control the details of the water, as well as regulating light-to-dark and in-focus-to-blur, by adding it rather than subtracting it. The sequence of events in this image are: first there is no wave, then the wave crashes, and then it recedes (**Figure 6.5a**).

FIGURE 6.5A *Before adding the first layer of water.*

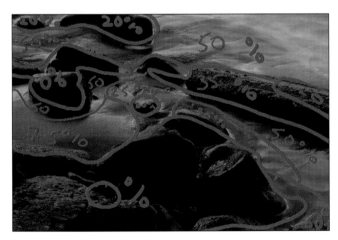

FIGURE 6.5B *The image map.*

Now that you have started building the foundation of the movement, it's time to build in the crescendo of the crashing wave while further reinforcing your choices about light-to-dark and in-focus-to-blur (**Figures 6.5b**, **6.5c**, and **6.5d**). Just as you did in the previous step, you will make your decisions with that in mind.

FIGURE 6.5C *After brushing in the water.*

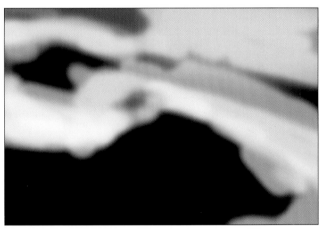

FIGURE 6.5D *The layer mask.*

FIGURE 6.6A *Before.*

FIGURE 6.6B *Image map for the IN layer.*

FIGURE 6.6C *After.*

FIGURE 6.6D *The layer mask.*

5. Make the IN layer active. Fill the layer mask with black, and brush in the water (**Figures 6.6a**, **6.6b**, **6.6c**, and **6.6d**).

Now you are going to further build up depth by creating a series of layers that range from very defined detail to less-defined detail. By doing this, you will achieve greater dimension in the water's mist.

6. Make the TEXTURE layer active. Fill the layer mask with black, and brush in the rocks (**Figures 6.7a**, **6.7b**, **6.7c**, and **6.7d**).

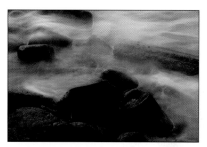

FIGURE 6.7A *Before.*

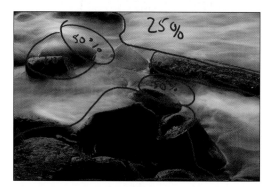

FIGURE 6.7B *The image map layer.*

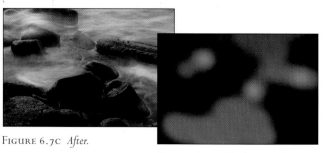

FIGURE 6.7C *After.*

FIGURE 6.7D *The layer mask.*

FIGURE 6.8A *Before.*

FIGURE 6.8B *The OUT copy image map.*

FIGURE 6.8C *After.*

FIGURE 6.8D *The layer mask.*

7. Make the IN/OUT copy the active layer. Move this layer so it is above the TEXTURE layer. Fill the layer mask with black, and brush in the water (**Figures 6.8a**, **6.8b**, **6.8c**, and **6.8d**).

8. Duplicate the TEXTURE layer and move the copy on top of the IN/OUT copy layer.

What you now have is a layer of sharp above a layer of blur, then sharp, then blur, and then sharp. By building the image this way, and varying the opacity of the sharp and blur layers, you give the image a three-dimensional quality that using only one layer can't achieve.

NOTE: As it turns out, you did not need the IN copy layer other than to use it (if you chose to) as a reference. So if you want to, you can discard it, which is what I did. I left it in the 100-ppi file, however, for consistency.

9. Next, do "The Move," create a master layer, and name it MASTER 1.

For CS2 and above, press and hold Ctrl-Alt-Shift-E/Cmd-Option-Shift-E. For CS and below, press Ctrl-Alt-Shift/Cmd-Option-Shift, then type N and then E.

10. Save the file as SMOKE 16bit.psd.

Step 2: Correct Color Cast

Now that you have one image, you can address the second-biggest issue, which is the overall color cast.

1. Using the Threshold adjustment layer approach, which we have done in every chapter except Chapter 5, find the black and white points of the image. (See "The Threshold Way to Correct Color Cast," in Chapter 1.)

FIGURE 6.8E

2. Create a BP Curves adjustment layer to correct the black point and a WP Curves adjustment layer to correct the white point. This is where I placed what will be the black and white point sample points (**Figure 6.8e**).

NOTE: If you're looking for the black and white points in the 100-ppi file, you'll notice that, although there are four sample points defined, none of them marks the black point. I will further discuss this issue under Step 5: Black-and-White Conversion.

3. Create a master layer, name it MASTER 2, and save the file (**Figures 6.8f** and **6.8g**).

Before I move on to adding selective sharpening and contrast to the image, you should notice that I have not run the Nik Skylight filter. The Nik Skylight filter is used to remove the blue cast that is inherent in shadow and, to varying degrees, in sunlight. However, because water is blue, if I correct for blue cast, the image will be reddish-brown and I will see more of the sand underneath the waves than I want. So in this instance, I will leave the blue cast and use it to my advantage. (RGB is a formula to mix color.) Here is what the image looked like both before and after I ran the filter (**Figures 6.8h** and **6.8i**).

FIGURE 6.8F *Before.*

FIGURE 6.8H *With Nik Skylight filter.*

FIGURE 6.8I *Without Nik Skylight filter.*

FIGURE 6.8G *After setting the black and white points.*

FIGURE 6.9A *Before.*

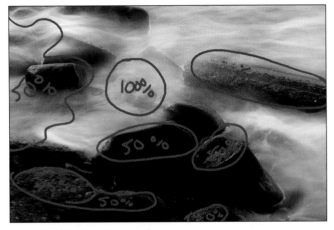

FIGURE 6.9B *Image map.*

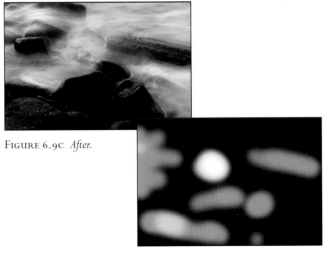

FIGURE 6.9C *After.*

FIGURE 6.9D *Layer mask.*

Step 3: Selective Sharpness and Selective Contrast

1. Duplicate the MASTER 2 layer twice. Name the first layer CONTRAST and the second layer SHARPEN. Make the CONTRAST layer active and hide the SHARPEN layer. Using the Nik Contrast Only filter, boost the contrast in a visually appealing way. The settings that I used were in the Basic menu: I left the Saturation at its default of 50%, Brightness at 55%, and Contrast at 60%. In the Advanced menu, I left the Protect Highlights at default 0% and the Protect Shadows at 30% (**Figures 6.9a**, **6.9b**, **6.9c**, and **6.9d**).

NOTE: Remember that with the Nik filter, you can protect the shadows and highlights as well as adjust the saturation.

2. Make the SHARPEN layer active and launch the Nik Sharpener Pro software. After you decide what parts of the image are important and where you want the viewer's unconscious eye to go, use it to selectively sharpen the image (**Figures 6.10a**, **6.10b**, **6.10c**, and **6.10d**).

NOTE: Because I wanted the viewer's eye to go first to the center rock, I made it the sharpest. To further force the eye to move to this central area, I also sharpened the sides of the dark rocks that face the center one.

Refer to the "How to Sharpen" Steps in Chapter 2. If you do not have the Nik Sharpener Pro software, look back at the section in Chapter 2 on how to sharpen in the LAB color space. If you have the Nik Sharpener Pro software, my settings were: for Printer—Type Epson Ink Jet, Printer resolution—2880 × 1440, and Paper Type—Textured and Fine Art. I left the image dimensions alone. Under Advanced, I used the eyedropper to select different shades of gray ranging from light to very dark. I did not change the black sample box. I chose not to sharpen the whites, so that I would not run the risk of blowing out the highlights. Sharpening by color is an approach that allows me very granular control over my image.

3. Turn on the CONTRAST layer (Click the Eyeball on.) and this is what you should see (**Figure 6.10e**).

FIGURE 6.10A *Before.*

FIGURE 6.10B *Image map.*

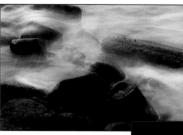

FIGURE 6.10C *After.*

FIGURE 6.10D *Layer mask.*

FIGURE 6.10E *Combined Sharpness and Contrast layers.*

Step 4: Light-to-Dark, Dark-to-Light, and Render Lighting

Why I chose to address the building up of the light-to-dark relationship of this image at this point, instead of closer to the beginning of the manipulations, is based on what I know about contrast and sharpness. Contrast is the difference in brightness between the light and dark areas of a picture. If there is a large difference between them, then the result is an image with high contrast. Therefore, by increasing the contrast, I can also darken and lighten the image. To a lesser degree, the same is true for sharpening. Sharpening, or un-sharp masking, an image creates the illusion of sharpness by adding contrast to pixel edges.

When I first began mapping this image, I knew that I would make it a black-and-white one, one of high contrast with deep, textured blacks (Zone II) and textured whites (Zone IX). Even though this image is fairly monochromatic and destined to be a continuous-tone black-and-white one, it still has all of its "color." Keeping in mind that RGB is not a color, it's a formula for mixing color, you are going to build up the relationship of light-to-dark, just as you built up the illusion of depth in the master layer.

FIGURE 6.11A *Before.*

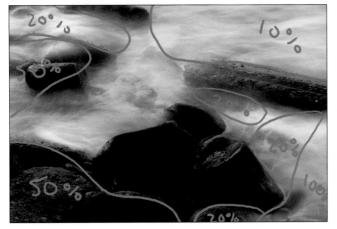

FIGURE 6.11B *Image map.*

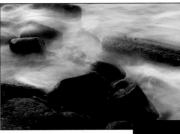

FIGURE 6.11C *After.*

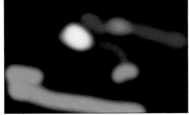

FIGURE 6.11D *The layer mask.*

To do this, you will use three separate blending modes with the Curves adjustment layers that you are about to create. The first Curves adjustment layer will use the blending mode Multiply. As we have discussed previously, the Multiply blending mode doubles the density of the image and increases the saturation in relationship to the increase in density. In this instance, that is a benefit instead of a detriment, because we aim to deepen the blacks while maintaining their detail. The second Curves adjustment layer will use the blending mode Luminosity, which affects only the light-to-dark aspect of the image and not the color or saturation. The last Curves adjustment layer that you will create will use the blending mode Normal. Normal, like Multiply, increases the saturation of the image, but Multiply doubles its density. You don't want to go very far with this adjustment.

NOTE: The three adjustment layer choices that we are about to make are the outcome of working with this image. The only decisions that were made beforehand were to darken the image after adjusting the contrast and sharpening, and to use the Multiply blending mode approach to darken the image with the first Curves adjustment layer. The other steps were taken to achieve the effect of light-to-dark so that I could re-create my original vision of this image.

The Multiply Blending Mode Light-to-Dark Adjustment layer

1. Create a Curves adjustment layer, click OK, and name it L2D MULTI.

2. Select Multiply as the blending mode, fill the adjustment layer with black, and paint with white at varying levels of opacity. These figures illustrate what I did (**Figures 6.11a, 6.11b**, **6.11c**, and **6.11d**).

FIGURE 6.12A *Before.*

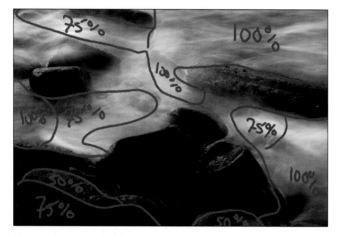

FIGURE 6.12B *Image map.*

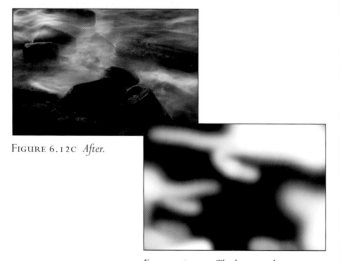

FIGURE 6.12C *After.*

FIGURE 6.12D *The layer mask.*

The Luminosity Blending Mode
Light-to-Dark Adjustment Layer

NOTE: When you chose the Multiply blending mode, you made decisions about color. Now you will, selectively, further darken areas in the image that you already darkened in a previous adjustment layer. In order to accomplish this without increasing the saturation, you will use the Luminosity blending mode.

1. Create a Curves adjustment layer.

2. Click on the center point, and drag it until the image is darkened. Do *not* pull the center point to where you clip or flatten the top or bottom of the curve. Click OK. Select Luminosity as the blending mode, fill the adjustment layer with black, and paint with white at varying levels of opacity. These figures illustrate what I did (**Figures 6.12a**, **6.12b**, **6.12c**, and **6.12d**).

The Normal Blending Mode
Light-to-Dark Adjustment layer

1. Create a Curves adjustment layer.

2. Click on the center point and drag it until the image is darkened, but without clipping either end of the curve. Leave the blending mode at Normal. Fill the adjustment layer with black and paint with white at varying levels of opacity. This illustrates what I did (**Figures 6.13a**, **6.13b**, **6.13c**, and **6.13d**).

3. Create a master layer, name it MASTER 3, and save the file. Now convert the file to 8 bit (Image > Mode > 8bit), and save it as SMOKE 8bit.psd.

The Render Lighting Effects Layer

A believable probability is better than an improbable believability. In order to create a believable probability, you must mimic reality; i.e., if light comes from one direction, you must create corresponding shadows that follow that direction. In this use of the Render lighting filter, you will place both light and dark where you want them and at the intensity you desire.

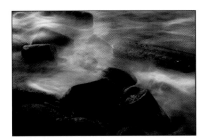

FIGURE 6.13A *Before.*

FIGURE 6.13B *Image map.*

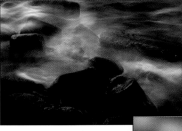

FIGURE 6.13C *After.*

FIGURE 6.13D *The layer mask.*

NOTE: Remember, this filter can be used to add darkness to an image as well as to add light. Thus, you can brush in darkness to increase an image's apparent lightness.

1. Duplicate the MASTER 3 layer and rename it LIGHTING.

2. Go to Filter > Render > Lighting Effects. The lighting choice from the Styles menus is Soft Omni. Assuming that you agree with my choice of the rock as the focus of this image, place the center point of the light on the center of the rock.

3. Click on the top anchor point and reduce the size of the light by dragging it so that the top anchor point is just inside the top of the image.

You are now going to change the color of the light. Because water is blue, we want to reinforce the decision we made in Step 2, which was *not* to remove the blue color cast of the image. That means that any light we add to the image should have some form of blueness to it as well.

4. Double-click on the white box located to the right of the Intensity slider in the Light type dialog box. This brings up the Color Picker dialog box. Click on the blue part of the spectrum on the color selector slider located next to the larger color box. (Make note of the Hue value, which for my selection was 222. It's OK if your RGB values are different than R: 204, G: 204, and B: 204; they are not active. **Figure 6.13e.**) Click OK.

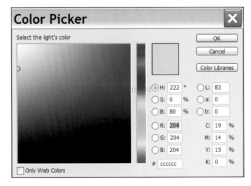

FIGURE 6.13E

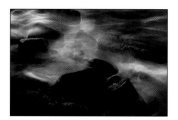

FIGURE 6.14A *Before.*

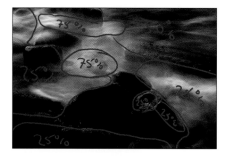

FIGURE 6.14B *Image map.*

FIGURE 6.14C *After applying Lighting Effects.*

FIGURE 6.14D *After brushwork and lowering layer opacity.*

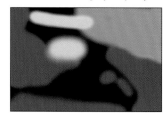

FIGURE 6.14E *The layer mask.*

5. Double-click on the white box in the Exposure dialog box, which brings up the Color Picker again, and type in the RGB values R: 204, G: 204, and B: 204. This is so that the ambient light will match the color of the light source's light. The settings that I finally settled on were Intensity 85, Gloss –72, Material 100, Exposure –68, and Ambience 89. The final adjustment that I made was to lower the LIGHTING layer's opacity to 70% (**Figures 6.14a**, **6.14b**, **6.14c**, **6.14d**, and **6.14e**).

NOTE: Because of the challenges that the size of the preview creates, it is a good idea to save what you are doing as a default and dial in the look you want.

Diminishing Contrast Using a Curves Adjustment Layer

After applying the Render > Lighting Effects filter, a hot spot has appeared in the upper left corner and the upper midpoint of the image. To diminish it, I suggest that you break a sacred Photoshop rule, "Thou shalt not clip a curve." You will lower the contrast and darken the area in question with a Curves adjustment layer by "clipping" the upper part of the curve.

1. Create a Curves adjustment layer. (Make sure your Curves dialog box is set to display the finer, 10-point grid, rather than the coarse, 4-point grid. Alt/Option-click the grid to switch between them.)

2. Click on the uppermost point of the curve and lower the upper curve anchor point by one grid mark. This lowers the contrast. Click on the center of the curve and drag the center point downward, on a diagonal, one grid point. This slightly darkens the image. The input value should be around 151 and the Output value around 99. Click OK, select the blending mode Luminosity, and name the adjustment layer LWR CONTRAST LUM. Fill the layer mask with black, then brush in the darkened, lowered contrast (**Figures 6.15a**, **6.15b**, **6.15c**, and **6.15d**).

FIGURE 6.15A *Before: The area that needs to be darkened and have its contrast lowered.*

FIGURE 6.15B *Image map.*

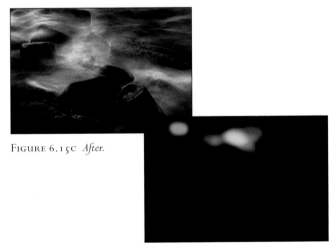

FIGURE 6.15C *After.*

FIGURE 6.15D *The layer mask.*

Step 5: Black-and-White Conversion

As soon as I harvested the first of the captures that comprise this image, I visualized the final print as a continuous-tone black-and-white one. All of the issues of contrast, sharpness, and color, as well as how this image was constructed, were addressed with this in mind. As you observed in the previous chapter, there is a relationship between red, green, and blue when it comes to converting an image from color to a continuous-tone black-and-white one. Also, as we discovered in the previous chapter, you can change the image dramatically by changing the order of the Channel Mixer layers. By changing the layer order, the contrast changes. The Channel Mixer layers are also adjustment layers, which means that they have layer masks, giving you exceptional control over the relationship of Red, Green, and Blue.

The steps for a basic black-and-white conversion are:

a. Analyze the image using a Hue/Saturation adjustment layer (by bringing the saturation slider to 100%).

b. Note the major color components. (You may want to address some issues in the image after converting the image to black-and-white by increasing/decreasing the saturation and darkness/lightness of the colors in the image.)

c. By shift-clicking on the potential highlight problem areas, place sample points. (Remember to bring the saturation slider to 0% when you are done.)

d. Create the Channel Mixer adjustment layer for the Green channel. Select Green from the Output Channel menu, then click Monochrome.

e. Modify the sliders until the image looks appealing. (Make sure that your sample points fall between 244 and 247, but try to keep as close to 244 as possible.)

f. Repeat Steps d and e for the Red channel and then the Blue channel.

g. If you intend to do brushwork on all three of the Channel Mixer layers that were created in the basic, black-and-white conversion, create a fourth Channel Mixer layer. In that layer, assign the values of 33 Red, 33 Green, 33 Blue, and a Constant of 1.

When it comes to fine-tuning an image, this is the way that I work. Once I have done the basic conversion, I look at each Channel Mixer layer individually and make note of what I like best about each one. Then, I observe the changes that occur as I change the layer stack order, again noting what I like and dislike. (For this image, from bottom to top, I prefer this order: Blue, Red, Green.)

NOTE: As I discussed in Chapter 5, a black-and-white conversion using a multiple Channel Mixer approach starts with Green (luminance), then Red (generally the lighter aspect of the tonal range of the image), then Blue (generally the darker end of the tonal range of an image). But your choices will depend on the colors in any given image. If an image is mostly blue, the green and red channels will appear to be darker, and so on. Case in point—in this image, I chose not to remove the blue cast, because I wanted to enhance the water. Water is blue. If I corrected for the blue cast, the image would be reddish-brown, and I would see more of the sand underneath the waves than I wanted.

Also, during this conversion, I used all four of the sample points that Photoshop allows. This means that, during the CCD color-cast correction, I had to move the sample point that I used for finding the black point of this image. I moved the black sample point from where it was in the rocks to where it is now on the center rock, which is the visual focus point of this image. I then laid down two more sample points in areas that looked to me like they might be problematic. Once you decide what area of an image is most important (e.g., the model's face over the bear's face in the first part of Chapter 5), one of the sample points becomes the most critical. It is that sample point on which I base my decisions. It is not important that all the sample points hit 244–247.

It's now time to selectively change the dynamics of the way red, green, and blue relate to each other by painting on the layer masks. This approach replicates the black-and-white, darkroom two-step development process mentioned earlier in the book. (See the sidebar "Doing the Developer Two-Step" in Chapter 5.) A two-step development process done traditionally was tedious, time-consuming, and expensive, but it produced the best tonal range to be had out of a print. The next series of steps you're going to take will replicate that process, but more accurately than you could in a traditional darkroom, and without your having to inhale all those chemicals. I know of no other way of converting a black-and-white image that affords you so much control. In this image, you will be working on all three Channel Mixer layers, so you will need to create a fourth, or Neutral, one.

Creating and Moving Sample Points

How you create a new sample point is first, you select the eyedropper from the Tools palette (keyboard command "I") and select the color sample tool, which is the second tool in that pull-down menu. (You can scroll through any tool by holding down the Shift key and clicking the letter that is that tool's keyboard command.) Holding the Shift key down, you click on the area in which you want to place a sample point. Keep in mind that Photoshop allows for no more than four sample points.

How you move an existing sample point is by again selecting the color sample tool and simply Shift-clicking on the sample point you want to move and then dragging it to the new area in which you want to place a sample point.

NOTE: The numbers I came up with for this image are:

Green CM layer: R: +9, G: +90, B: +10, Constant –3

Red CM layer: R: +83, G: +4, B: +14, Constant –2

Blue CM layer: R: +10, G: +17, B: +74, Constant 0

The images printed in this book are too small to adequately show the subtlety of what was done. Therefore, after you do the next step, find the layer set in the 100-ppi SMOKE file entitled C M LAYERS UNTOUCHED. Take a look at this file, which contains the layers before the layer masks were modified.

Make active whatever you decided would be your top Channel Mixer layer. Create a new Channel Mixer layer, check the Monochrome box, and type in 33 for Red, 33 for Green, 33 for Blue, and 1 for Constant. Click OK. Name this layer NEUTRAL.

NOTE: This adds a little density and allows you to work on all three of the other Channel Mixer layers without worrying that there might be some color bleed in an area where all three layers were worked on. We did the same thing in the second, advanced black-and-white conversion method in Chapter 5.

This is what the image looks like after the basic Green, Red, Blue Channel Mixer conversions (**Figure 6.16a**).

This is what the image looks like after the Channel Mixer order is changed to Blue-Red-Green (**Figure 6.16b**).

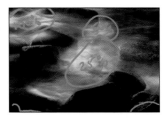

FIGURE 6.17A *Blue image map.*

FIGURE 6.17B *The layer mask.*

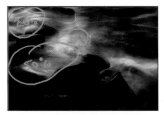

FIGURE 6.17C *Red image map.*

FIGURE 6.17D *The layer mask.*

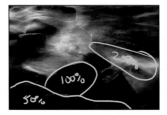

FIGURE 6.17E *Green image map.*

FIGURE 6.17F *The layer mask.*

FIGURE 6.18 *After adjusting the layer masks.*

This is what the three image maps look like (**Figures 6.17a, 6.17c**, and **6.17e**).

After you adjust the layer masks (shown in **Figures 6.17b, 6.17d**, and **6.17f**), this is what you have (**Figure 6.18**).

Addressing Issues of Dark-to-Light Using a Curves Adjustment Layer

So far, every choice you have made has dealt with the light-to-dark aspect of the image. In this step, you will explore the dark-to-light aspect. It is important to remember that darkness is as important to an image as lightness. The use of dark isolates can have as much impact as the use of light ones.

1. Create a Curves adjustment layer. (Make sure your Curves dialog box is set to display the finer, 10-point grid.)

2. Click on the center point and darken the image by dragging it, on the diagonal, by one grid line. Click OK and name this layer D 2 L NORM. Because you want to reveal, and not conceal 80% of what you have just done, leave the layer mask white, and paint with black. Now, paint the areas of the rocks that are too dark by painting back in some lightness (**Figures 6.19a**, **6.19b**, **6.19c**, and **6.19d**).

In the course of everything you have done to this image, some of the texture detail in the foreground rocks has been lost. As we have talked about several times previously, in the Zone System, Zone IX is textured white (244–247) and Zone II is textured black. To retrieve the detail in the Zone II areas of this image, you are again going to break the sacred "Thou shalt not clip a curve" Photoshop rule.

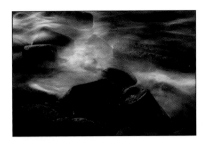

FIGURE 6.19A *Before.*

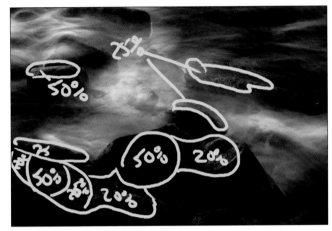

FIGURE 6.19B *Dark-to-light image map.*

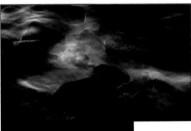

FIGURE 6.19C *After.*

FIGURE 6.19D *The layer mask.*

NOTE: When it comes to global adjustments, you never want to clip a curve. But in this instance, you are targeting a very small area for which, regardless of how much care you took in the editing process up to this point, you would still find yourself dealing with more or less the same issue. You don't need to worry about what will happen to the highlights; you will be masking them. What you need to do is open the shadows, which you will be allowing through your mask. Be careful of making things dogma. Solve the problem at hand; don't assume that a tool's limitation is not also the tool's power.

3. Make the NEUTRAL layer the active one. (You want this Curve to be under the D 2 L NORM adjustment layer.) Create a Curves adjustment layer, click on the control point, and move the curve until it looks like this (**Figure 6.20**). Click OK and name it ROCKS.

What you should be looking at is this (**Figure 6.21**).

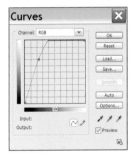

FIGURE 6.20 *Deliberately clipping the ROCKS curve.*

FIGURE 6.21 *The high-contrast result of clipping the curve.*

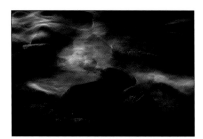

FIGURE 6.22A *Before.*

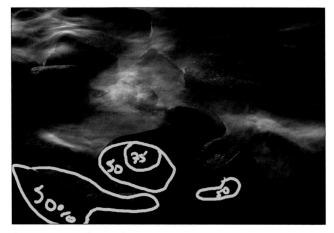

FIGURE 6.22B *Image map.*

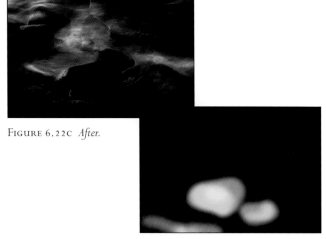

FIGURE 6.22C *After.*

FIGURE 6.22D *The layer mask.*

4. Fill the layer mask with black and brush back the foreground rocks (**Figures 6.22a**, **6.22b**, **6.22c**, and **6.22d**).

Step 6: Fixing a Concrete Problem

By now, you know that a good, dynamic workflow habit is to always give yourself an exit strategy. Initially, I thought that the broken piece of the concrete Coast Guard pier was important, but after the image was converted and a print was made, the concrete piece distracted from the central focus point of the image. Because I had built in an exit strategy, I could reach back to the beginning and use the original source layers to correct the problem. (If I had flattened this image, I'd have been out of luck.)

NOTE: In this image's original workflow, the file was saved as a 16-bit layered Photoshop Document file (.psd), the file was then flattened, converted to 8-bit, and saved as SMOKE 8bit.psd. My work with the image went on from there. Later, I had to reopen the 16-bit file and convert it to 8-bit in order to address the issues that arose after the image was first printed. To save time and streamline the efficiency of this lesson, I suggested that you convert the entire file to 8-bit.

The issue confronting you now is that all of the layers that you need are color ones, so before you can remove the unwanted piece of concrete pier, you need to convert the color layers that you want to use into continuous-tone black-and-white.

1. Move the IN copy layer that you duplicated in the beginning to just below the LWR CONTRAST layer, and fill the layer mask with white. Make the D 2 L NORM layer active, make a master layer, and call it CORRECTION 3. Create a layer mask and fill it with black. Turn the layer off and discard the IN copy layer. You no longer need it. This layer is in color, and you have just created the black-and-white version that you need.

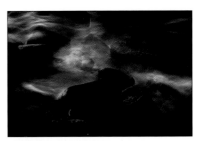

FIGURE 6.23A *Before.*

FIGURE 6.23B *Image map.*

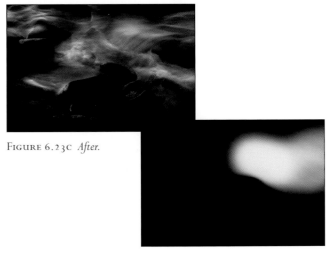

FIGURE 6.23C *After.*

FIGURE 6.23D *The layer mask.*

2. Duplicate the IN/OUT layer, move it to just below the LWR CONTRAST layer, and fill the layer mask with white. Make D 2 L NORM the active layer, create a master layer, and call this one CORRECTION 2. Create a layer mask and fill it with black. Turn the layer off and discard the duplicate of the IN/OUT layer.

3. Duplicate the LIGHTING layer. Fill the layer mask with white. Move this layer to just below the LWR CONTRAST layer. Make the D 2 L NORM layer active, create a master layer, and call it CORRECTION 1. Create a layer mask and fill it with black. Turn the layer off and discard the duplicate of the LIGHTING layer.

You created correction layers in a particular order based on the decision to capture motion with stillness. Thus, you want the motion of the water, the CORRECTION 3 layer (the IN layer copy), to be primary. The more diffused CORRECTION 2 layer (the IN/OUT layer copy) will be the underpinning of the final image, while the light and dark image structures of the CORRECTION 1 layer (the LIGHTING layer copy) will provide the finishing touches.

4. Make CORRECTION 3 the active layer and brush it so that it looks something like this (**Figures 6.23a**, **6.23b**, **6.23c**, and **6.23d**).

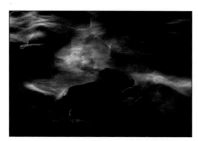

FIGURE 6.24A *Before.*

FIGURE 6.24B *Image map.*

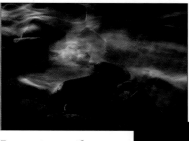

FIGURE 6.24C *After.*

FIGURE 6.24D *The layer mask.*

5. Make CORRECTION 2 the active layer and brush it so that it looks something like this (**Figures 6.24a**, **6.24b**, **6.24c**, and **6.24d**).

6. Make CORRECTION 3 the active layer and brush it so that it looks something like the final image (**Figures 6.25a**, **6.25b**, **6.25c**, **6.25d**, and **6.25e**).

7. Duplicate the D 2 L NORM adjustment layer, move it above the CORRECTION 3 layer, and lower the opacity to 50%. Make a master layer, name it MASTER FINAL, and save the file (**Figure 6.26**).

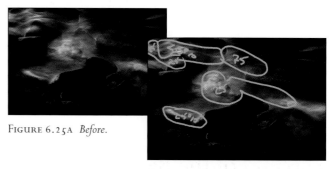

FIGURE 6.25A *Before.*

FIGURE 6.25B *Image map.*

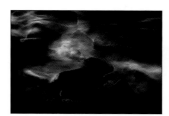

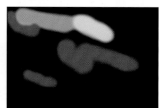

FIGURE 6.25C *After.*   FIGURE 6.25D *The layer mask.*

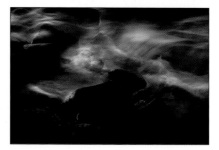

FIGURE 6.25E *All three correction layers combined.*

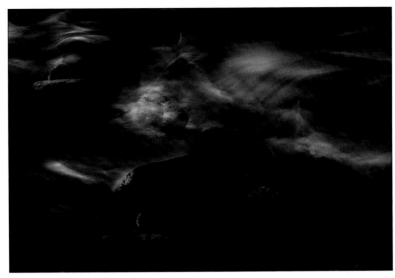

FIGURE 6.26 *The final* Smoke *image.*

The End of the Beginning

I never think of the future. It comes soon enough.

—Albert Einstein

Before you ever press the shutter, there must be something that moves you to do so. If you are not moved, you will not move others. See the image in your mind's eye in its completed form, and make your captures so that the experience of time will be an element in your final print. Then, when you take your captures to your computer, try to re-create your original vision, removing everything that doesn't conform to that vision. Do not try to make a memorable image out of a capture made casually, even if it was a happy accident.

If you have read all that has preceded this, you know that a still camera's limitations are also its power. John Paul Caponigro has said, "The camera is what I use to hold the world still." And this isn't "hold" in the sense of tying something down. That's too often the case with people who feel that all photographs must be posed and the subject must stay completely still. "Sit, move your head to left. … No, too much, okay, hold that. Place your hand under your chin. … Stop. … Hold that, don't move." Shooting that way produces images so devoid of life and time that they are eminently forgettable.

You should want to create images that feel as if they are about to move or were caught as if they were already in motion. I'll say it one more time: *A still photograph is called a still photograph because the picture doesn't move, not because the objects in the picture are not in motion.* You can capture motion with stillness and, in that moment, hold time still, but yet experience the feeling of its passing.

There is a quote often attributed to the philosopher Søren Kierkegaard: "Life must be lived forward, but can only be understood backward." If your final print encompasses the experience of life moving forward, that image will allow your viewer to understand it backward.

Afterword

When Vincent asked me to write this piece, I protested that I am anti-Photoshop and anti–post-shot manipulation, and generally I think it's all an excuse for slovenly thinking and seeing. Vincent said, "Fine, it's important for readers to know about all sides of the question."

He wrote a book, I get 500 words to express my opinion.

Photography is about vision. There is one major thing to remember after reading this book. Photoshop and other post-shot manipulations are corrections and addendums to your vision.

When I teach, I tell my students that the one phrase I don't want to hear is, "I can fix it in Photoshop." You are responsible for every square millimeter of your image at the time you shoot it.

I've often thought that the reason the grass always looks greener on the other side of the fence is because it's backlit. Truth then, depends on where you're standing and is thus quite subjective. Without getting into an intricate philosophical evaluation of truth, I'd like to quote the French painter, Georges Braque: "Truth exists, only falsehood has to be invented."

There may be times when your original concept will call for and include the use of post-shot manipulation. When that is a conscious decision made before the image is taken, you are no longer using it to correct an inferior or badly thought-out image. You are then using post-shot manipulation as an integral part of the process of seeing, and seeing and vision are of course the essence and reason for photography.

It is incumbent upon you to make sure you are getting what you want at the moment you take the picture. It would be best for you to spend more time thinking of the quality of your pictures and less time thinking about the quality of your pixels. The parameters of your vision are more important than the expertise you have with levels and curves or whatever you get involved with after you take the picture.

Your responsibility and obligation as a photographer lies with your concept and execution at the instant of exposure. I have seen so many demonstrations that dealt with the correction of an inferior image that I want to shout out, "Screw the corrections, do it right in the first place or do it over until you get it right." Don't depend on post-shot manipulation as a crutch. It will only make you sloppy in your execution of the image.

The American playwright Arthur Miller said that he tried to create the poem from the evidence. I wish you to see not how clever you can be, but how observant you can be. The reality that is out there is rich and varied and worthy of investigation. The search into the real world can, with insight, lead not merely to replication, but revelation.

This is not to say that you cannot enhance the vision that you have, rather to reiterate that you must discipline yourself to be responsible to and have faith in your original vision.

Ernst Haas once said, "We do not take pictures, we are taken by pictures." He also said something else that took me a long time to understand. I don't remember the exact words, but it was something like, don't work so hard to take a picture. Years later I understood, and wrote a poem for my students that I think encompasses what he meant about working so hard to make it work and also illustrates the passion I think is of utmost importance:

If it doesn't excite you,
the thing that you see,
then why in the world
would it excite me?

—Jay Maisel

Index